LAW, PSYCHOLOGY, AND DEATH PENALTY LITIGATION

James R. Eisenberg

Professional Resource Press
Sarasota, Florida

Published by
Professional Resource Press
(An Imprint of the Professional Resource Exchange, Inc.)
Post Office Box 15560
Sarasota, FL 34277-1560

Printed in the United States of America

Copyright © 2004
Professional Resource Exchange, Inc.

The copy editor for this book was David Anson, the managing editor was Debbie Fink, the production coordinator was Laurie Girsch, and the text and cover designer was Deirdre DeLay.

Library of Congress Cataloging-in-Publication Data

Eisenberg, James R., date.
   Law, psychology, and death penalty litigation / James R. Eisenberg.
     p. cm.
   Includes bibliographical references and index.
   ISBN 1-56887-089-2 (alk. paper)
     1. Capital punishment--United States. 2. Sentences (Criminal procedure)--United States--Psychological aspects. 3. Criminal psychology--United States. 4. Extenuating circumstances--United States. I Title.

KF9227.C2E38 2004
345.73'0773--dc22

2004044609

DEDICATION

For Chris and Evelyn

PREFACE

In 1984, I received a call from the Office of the Ohio Public Defender to assist them on "mitigation" in a death penalty case. I had no idea what they were talking about. Twenty years later I have come to appreciate the complexities of death penalty litigation and have developed a deep respect for those psychologists and attorneys and other mental health professionals who have devoted much of their professional lives to this work. This project began over 10 years ago when Alan Goldstein invited me to present a workshop on the Role of the Psychologist in Death Penalty Litigation. His leadership in directing an outstanding continuing education program for the American Academy of Forensic Psychology (AAFP) is an inspiration for all of us who have participated in and taken these workshops. I have always appreciated the opportunity to present for AAFP but more importantly to learn from other presenters. I am indebted to my colleagues from the American Board of Forensic Psychology.

There are a number of individuals who assisted me during the process of turning this manuscript into a better book. Jeffrey Smalldon (a former English teacher) spared no red ink as he meticulously scoured several chapters. Mary Connell was particularly helpful with her insights on some of the ethical problems inherent in death penalty litigation. I am especially thankful to Mark Cunningham for his invaluable critical analysis and substantive contributions to my manuscript. I am also thankful to Dennis Stevens, Dean of Academic Affairs at Lake Erie College, for his support and his interest in this project. I am grateful to Lake Erie College for granting me a sabbatical in order to write this book.

In addition to those listed above, the following individuals made significant contributions towards the completion of this project: Dan Anker, PhD, LLD; Maria Bagshaw; Maria de la Camara, PhD; Phyllis

Crocker, Esquire; Susan Culotta and The Honorable Vincent Culotta; David Doughten, Esquire; Evelyn Eisenberg; The Honorable Carolyn Friedland; Joanne Gurley, Esquire; Marsha Hedrick, PhD; Kirk Heilbrun, PhD; Marge Koosed, Esquire; Sandra Lockett; Sarah Lovett; Susan Marshall, PhD; Jay Milano, Esquire; Phillip Resnick, MD; Tom Sartini, Esquire; Joyce Yachanin; and Robert Whitely.

I want to give a special "thanks" to Larry Ritt, Debra Fink, and the rest of the staff at Professional Resource Press for their support for this project from the very beginning. I am grateful for their dedication and commitment to professional publications.

Most of all thanks to my wife, Chris DiCello.

TABLE OF CONTENTS

LAW, PSYCHOLOGY, AND DEATH PENALTY LITIGATION

James R. Eisenberg

Chapter 1

INTRODUCTION

In 1972, the Supreme Court ruled that the death penalty in its current form was unconstitutional, thus vacating the death sentences of everyone on death row (*Furman v. Georgia*). Following the reinstatement of the death penalty in 1976 (*Gregg v. Georgia*), several Supreme Court decisions resulted in psychologists and other forensic mental health specialists taking on an increasingly important role in capital litigation. Both in *Eddings v. Oklahoma* and *Lockett v. Ohio* the Supreme Court held that death penalty schemes must allow for consideration as a mitigating factor any aspect of the defendant's character or record and any of the circumstances of the offense that the defendant offers as a basis for a sentence less than death. Given that the imposition of death by public authorities "is so profoundly different from all other penalties" (*Lockett*), the Court ruled that an individualized decision is essential in capital cases. Thus, the need for treating each defendant in a capital case with that degree of respect due the uniqueness of the individual is far more important than in noncapital cases. In *Ake v. Oklahoma*, the Court held that the due process clause requires that an indigent defendant whose sanity or future dangerousness may be a significant factor in trial or sentencing must be provided access to a psychiatrist's assistance on this issue to gather facts, present testimony, and assist in preparing the cross-examination of the state's witnesses. The failure to request the assistance of mental health experts (psychologists, psychiatrists, social workers, mitigation specialists) could be a basis for a later finding of ineffective assistance of counsel (see *Strickland v. Washington*). The *Wiggins v. Smith* decision affirms that attorneys must conduct a thorough mitigation investigation that would normally include a psychological evaluation of a defendant especially into the nature and extent of abuse.

These cases are often used as the legal basis for appointing mental health professionals to assist in the defense of capital cases. Of course, prosecutors and district attorneys can hire their own mental health professionals to rebut the testimony of the experts called by the defendants. In jurisdictions where "future dangerousness" is a consideration (see *Jurek v. Texas*) mental health experts are likely to be called to address that issue at sentencing.

The purpose of this book is to assist psychologists and other forensic professionals in the preparation necessary for work on a capital case. Advanced undergraduate and graduate students may also find the information useful. This book should serve as a guide covering the essentials from case law to the practical aspects of the forensic evaluation. Chapter 2, A Brief History of the Death Penalty, provides a brief discussion of the history and evolution of the death penalty, with particular emphasis on the Eighth Amendment and some examples of the "trials of the century." Chapter 3, Significant U.S. Supreme Court Decisions in Capital Cases Since 1970, covers the decisions that have some impact on psychological or psychiatric testimony and preparation. Chapter 4, Stages of a Capital Case, presents the lengthy appellate process in capital cases and why psychological evaluations may be requested at any time from pretrial to "execution." Chapter 5, Aggravating and Mitigating Factors and Jury Instructions, is a summary of the typical statutory requirements for indicting a defendant with a capital crime and those factors that a jury may consider in recommending a sentence other than death. Chapter 6, Mitigation, provides a more detailed discussion of mitigation and an analysis of the *Lockett v. Ohio* decision. Chapter 7, Getting Started on a Capital Case, is a discussion of how one initially becomes involved in a death penalty trial, with emphasis on practical matters. Chapter 8, The Role of the Psychologist in Death Penalty Litigation, looks at the various roles that psychologists or psychiatrists play in capital litigation. Chapter 9, Special Issues: Competency, Sanity, and the Death Penalty, summarizes the standards used for such assessments and the legal implications. Chapter 10, Mental Retardation and the Death Penalty, is a discussion of the specific issues associated with mental retardation and a review of the Supreme Court Decision (*Atkins v. Virginia*) that lays the legal foundation for such evaluations. Chapter 11, The Antisocial Personality Disorder, Psychopathy, and Risk Assessment, examines the history, etiology, and other issues associated with the antisocial personality disorder and how it is a factor in many capitally charged defendants. Chapter 12, Case Study: Boo and Rail Do a Lick, is an example of a capital case to be used for discussion of many of the issues raised at trial and mitigation. Chapter 13, Ethical Issues in Capital Litigation, reviews various ethical standards and discusses some of the inherent problems in death penalty evaluations. Appendix A, Key Areas to Explore in Defendant's

History, is a list of numerous issues for investigation in a defendant's life (see pp. 141-142). Finally, Appendix B is a compilation of death penalty facts provided by the Death Penalty Information Center and the National Association for the Advancement of Colored People (NAACP) Legal Defense Fund (see pp. 143-146).

When relevant, case histories are provided to highlight some of the legal or psychological issues. These case histories are drawn from my professional experiences and represent my perspective on psychological and legal issues.

Chapter 2

A BRIEF HISTORY OF
THE DEATH PENALTY

This chapter is designed to serve as a brief introduction to the history of the death penalty and a review of the Eighth Amendment. There are many excellent sources of information for a more thorough review of both of these areas. It is useful, however, when given a death penalty assignment to understand the historical perspective for capital punishment and the evolution of the death penalty in the United States. The Death Penalty Information Center (www.deathpenaltyinfo.org) provides an excellent review of the history as well as links to many relevant sites, statistics, court rulings, and position papers.

EARLY DEATH PENALTY LAWS

There are numerous references to capital punishment throughout recorded history. The first codified death penalty laws date to the eighteenth century B.C. in the Code of King Hammaurabi of Babylon (Reggio, 1997) with 25 different crimes eligible for the death penalty. Ironically, murder was not one of them. The death penalty was also part of the fourteenth century B.C.'s Hittite Code; in the seventh century B.C.'s Draconian Code of Athens, which made death the only punishment for all crimes; and in the fifth century B.C.'s Roman Law of the Twelve Tablets. Death sentences were carried out by such means as crucifixion, drowning, beating to death, burning alive, and impalement (Reggio, 1997).

Capital punishment is a penalty prescribed by Biblical law for the commission of offenses that violate ritual prohibitions (such as working on of the Sabbath; Exodus 35:2; all Biblical references are taken from the Holy Scriptures according to the Masoretic text, 1917) as well as laws regarding interpersonal relationships (murder, kidnapping, and incest). The Biblical text explicitly specifies two forms of execution: stoning (Exodus 17:4; Numbers 14:10) and burning (Leviticus 20:14, 21:9) as well as strangulation and decapitation (see amicus brief in *Bryan v. Moore*). Perhaps the first hint of the antisocial personality disorder and subsequent punishment (that included lynching) is found in the following:

> This our son is stubborn and rebellious, he doth not hearken to our voice; he is a glutton and a drunkard. And all the men of his city shall stone him with stones, that he die; so shalt thou put away the evil from the midst of thee; and all Israel shall hear, and fear. (Deuteronomy 21:20-21)

> And if a man have committed a sin worthy of death, and he be put to death, and thou hang him on a tree; his body shall not remain all night upon the tree, but thou shalt surely bury him the same day; for he that is hanged is a reproach unto God; that thou defile thy land which the Lord thy God giveth thee for an inheritance. (Deuteronomy 21:22)

In spite of the references to capital punishment, early Talmudic law required a careful review process that made capital punishment rare. For a Jew to be convicted by a Jewish court, two eyewitnesses must have seen the perpetrator about to commit the crime and warned him of the potential penalty. The murderer must verbally answer that he chooses to proceed anyway. (For a non-Jew, only one witness is required and no verbal warning.) Twenty-three, rather than the usual three judges, must sit on the rabbinical court, among other requirements; circumstantial evidence is never allowed in a Jewish court hearing a capital case (Pfefferman, 2003).

According to Laurence (1932), under the Roman republic, vestal virgins who violated their vows of chastity were buried alive. In the fifth century B.C., the following "crimes" were punishable by death: publishing libels and insulting songs, theft by a slave, perjury, willful murder of a freeman, and making disturbances in the city at night.

There are also numerous references to capital crimes through the Middle Ages until the modern era (see Banner, 2002; Bedau 1997; Costanzo & White, 1994; Latzer, 1998; Laurence, 1932; Randa, 1997; and the Death Penalty Information Center). In the sixteenth century, under the reign of Henry VIII, as many as 72,000 people are estimated to have been executed. Some common methods of execution at that time were boiling, burning at the stake, hanging, beheading, and drawing and quartering. Executions were carried out for such capital offenses as marrying a Jew, not confessing to a crime, and treason (Reggio,

1997). Randa (1997) reports that by 1700 the number of capital crimes in Britain rose to 222 (these death-eligible crimes included stealing, cutting down a tree, and robbing a rabbit warren).

In 1651, Thomas Hobbes (1588-1679) raised the argument that the purpose of punishment (contrary to the old Christian view) is not to teach people that it is immoral to commit murder, but to make it contrary to their interests. Capital punishment is necessary because it creates fear of the law in a way that life imprisonment does not. But because no individual ever gives up his or her right to self-preservation, the accused person (whether innocent or guilty) has a right to kill the jailer, the executioner, or anyone who aids these people. As soon as the law says that he or she must be put to death, all obligations under the social contract are null and void. Since we enter civil society for entirely selfish reasons, our obligations to it end when civil society fails to satisfy our interests (Berns, 1979).

THE DEATH PENALTY IN THE UNITED STATES

The early American colonies adopted most of their criminal laws, including the death penalty, from English Common Law. Kronenwetter (2001) reports that at one point every colony supported capital punishment. That included the offense of "cursing a parent" in the Massachusetts Bay Colony. The Bay Colony listed statutory rape, rebellion, adultery, buggery, idolatry, witchcraft, bestiality, man stealing, and blasphemy as capital crimes. The first recorded execution in the new colonies was that of Captain George Kendall in the Jamestown Colony of Virginia in 1608. Kendall was executed for being a spy for Spain (Randa, 1997).

The Constitution provided options for the death penalty for both the states and the Federal Government. Each state would then develop its own death penalty crimes. These varied greatly from one geographical area to another. Bedau (1997) reported that in the West and the South, horse thievery, claim jumping, and cattle rustling were hanging crimes. In the South, rape was a capital offense (and remained so until *Coker v. Georgia*). North Carolina's list of capital offenses included circulating seditious literature among slaves, inciting slaves to insurrection, stealing slaves, and harboring slaves for the purpose of setting them free. Virginia listed only five capital crimes for whites, but 70 for blacks (Costanzo & White, 1994).

The movement to restrict or abolish capital punishment in the United States started in the late 1700s and continued throughout the next two centuries. Pennsylvania restricted capital punishment to first degree murder in 1794 while Michigan became the first state to abolish the death penalty for all crimes in 1852 (Costanzo & White, 1994). Most states, however, continued to support capital punishment even though the number of individuals executed relative to the number of homicides had been consistently very small.

However, the total number of executions from 1608 to 1972 was 14,489 (Death Penalty Information Center; DPIC). The number of executions per year reached a peak in 1935 when 199 defendants were executed. These numbers declined steadily and were then halted in 1968 pending Supreme Court review. Following reinstatement of the death penalty the number of executions from 1976 to January of 2004 was 887 (DPIC). During this period of time the homicide rate varied from 10.2 per 100,000 population in 1980, to 7.9 per 100,000 in 1985, rising again to 9.8 per 100,000 in 1991, and then declining to 5.5 per 100,000 by 2000 (Bureau of Justice Statistics, 2003).

TRIALS OF THE CENTURY

One could argue that there were a number of "trials of the century" that influenced the support of the death penalty. Since 1900, a number of these famous trials have stimulated arguments both for and against capital punishment. In 1924, Nathan Leopold and Richard Loeb were convicted of murdering a neighborhood child. They were represented by Clarence Darrow and pled guilty to the charges and were given life sentences by the presiding judge. The film *Compulsion* is loosely based on their homicide and trial.

In 1920, two Italian anarchists, Nicola Sacco and Bartolomeo Vanzetti, were charged with robbing and killing a shoe factory employee in Boston. They were convicted and executed in 1925. The case resulted in international attention and debate about their guilt or innocence.

Certainly one of the true crimes and trials of the century occurred in 1932 with the kidnapping and murder of the 19-month-old son of Charles Lindbergh. Richard Hauptmann was convicted and 4 years later executed in New Jersey. Also in 1932, Kansas reinstated the death penalty following the multiple homicides of Bonnie Parker and Clyde Barrow.

Other noteworthy trials included those of Caryl Chessman, Ethel and Julius Rosenberg, Ted Bundy, and Timothy McVeigh. Caryl Chessman was accused of kidnapping and rape. He published four books while in prison and had considerable support throughout the country. He was executed in 1960, despite the attempts of Governor Edmund Brown to halt the execution. Ethel and Julius Rosenberg were executed in 1953 for espionage. It was claimed that they provided secret information about the atomic bomb to the Soviet Union. In 1989, the serial killer Ted Bundy was executed in Florida for the murders of Margaret Bowman, Lisa Levy, and Kimberly Leach. And more recently, Timothy McVeigh was executed in 2001 for the bombing of the Alfred P. Murrah Federal Building in Oklahoma City that resulted in the deaths of 168 people. Following the attacks on the World Trade Center and the Pentagon, terrorism was added as an aggravating factor in several states including Virginia, Tennessee, New Jersey, and Oklahoma. The trials of the "Snipers" John Mohammad and Lee Malvo were conducted, in part, under the terrorism statutes.

THE EIGHTH AMENDMENT
AND THE CONSTITUTIONALITY
OF THE DEATH PENALTY

The Eighth Amendment to the Constitution was ratified in 1791 and reads:

> Excessive bail shall not be required, nor excessive fines imposed, nor cruel and unusual punishments inflicted.

Latzer (1998) has provided a concise summary of the history of the Amendment and in particular the evolution of the "Cruel and Unusual Punishment Clause." Latzer states that the clause originates from the English Bill of Rights in 1689 in a response to the cruelty of King James II who executed hundreds of dissidents. Latzer states that the Cruel and Unusual Punishment Clause (as well as the specific wording of the Fifth Amendment) was not intended to abolish capital punishment, but was intended (in part) to forbid the infliction of more pain than was necessary to extinguish life and to prohibit such barbaric procedures as beheading and disemboweling. The Supreme Court, therefore, was faced with questions of "implementation" as opposed to questions of "constitutionality" of the death penalty.

The Supreme Court finally suspended the death penalty in 1968, pending a review of several cases (*Branch v. Texas; Furman v. Georgia;* and *Jackson v. Georgia*). In the 1972 *Furman* decision, the Court set aside all death penalty convictions on the grounds that under the current scheme, the punishment was "arbitrary and capricious" and "cruel and unusual" as it was implemented, thus violating the Eighth Amendment (see Chapter 3 for a summary of the *Furman* decision). The suspension of the death penalty, however, was temporary and was reinstated following the *Gregg v. Georgia* decision. The Court rejected the opinion that the death penalty was always unconstitutional. The Court held in *Gregg* that the Georgia (as well as the Florida) death penalty statute successfully overcame the problems of *Furman*, thus eliminating the unconstitutionality of unguided jury discretion and instituting other constitutional safeguards (narrowing the class of individuals eligible for the death penalty, providing appellate review, and mitigation). Therefore, the death penalty was constitutionally permissible again in 1976 and remains so today. The death penalty had been suspended from 1968 until the execution by firing squad of Gary Gilmore on January 17, 1977.

Today the death penalty is limited, with the exception of treason, to aggravated or first degree murder. In addition to the aggravated murder, the defendant must also be charged with and found guilty of the aggravating or special circumstances. Murder alone would not normally make one eligible for the death penalty. The bifurcated trial process requires that the jury first determine guilt or innocence (as well as determine if any aggravating circumstances exist) and, second, determine the appropriate sentence. Jurors may recommend the death penalty, but the final determination rests with the trial judge who can override a jury's recommendation for death and impose a life sentence. Prior to the *Ring v. Arizona* decision, three states (Alabama, Florida, and Indiana) allowed a judge to override a jury's recommendation for life and impose a death sentence.

There are a number of other important death penalty related issues that continue to be sources for research, review, and political discussion. These include the issues of race and the death penalty, the role of deterrence, jury selection (or what is sometimes referred to as the "death qualification" process), the cost of the death penalty, retribution, the execution of those who are mentally ill and mentally retarded, and the possible execution of those who are innocent. Some of these topics have been addressed before by the courts (such as race in *McCleskey v. Kemp;* jury selection in *Lockhart v. McCree* and *Wainwright v. Witt;* and mental retardation in *Atkins v. Virginia* and *Penry v. Lynaugh*) and may in the future serve as a basis for continued constitutional review under the "evolving standards of decency."

Chapter 3

SIGNIFICANT U.S. SUPREME COURT DECISIONS IN CAPITAL CASES SINCE 1970

BRIEF BACKGROUND

In 1972, the Supreme Court held in *Furman v. Georgia* that the states cannot impose the death penalty on a selected group of offenders in an arbitrary, capricious, or discriminatory manner based solely on the offense committed. The Court held that as a result of giving the jury unguided discretion to impose or not to impose the death penalty for murder, the penalty was being imposed discriminatorily, wantonly, freakishly, and so infrequently that any given death sentence was cruel and unusual. As a result, all death penalty cases were vacated and set for re-sentencing. Although the separate opinions by Justices Brennan and Marshall stated that the death penalty itself was unconstitutional, the overall holding in *Furman* was that the specific state death penalty statutes were unconstitutional. With that holding, the Court essentially delegated to the states to rewrite their death penalty statutes to eliminate the problems cited in *Furman*. Advocates of capital punishment began proposing new statutes that they believed would end arbitrariness in capital sentencing.

In 1976, the Supreme Court in *Gregg v. Georgia* re-examined the death penalty issue in the context of the Eighth Amendment. The Court ruled that the Eighth Amendment must be "interpreted in a flexible and dynamic manner" that reflects society's evolving standards of decency. It is that standard — "decency" — which is used by the Court in *Gregg* and more recently in *Atkins* (see below) to test the validity of a punishment under the Eighth Amendment. Since Georgia's legislature had narrowed the class of individuals eligible for the death penalty, the Court declared that no longer could a jury wantonly and freakishly impose the death sentence; it is always circumscribed by the legislative guidelines. The Court made clear "so long as the class of murderers subject to capital punishment is narrowed, there is no constitutional infirmity in a procedure that allows a jury to recommend mercy based on the mitigating evidence introduced by a defendant."

On the same day that the Court issued its landmark decision in *Gregg*, the Court decided four companion cases addressing the constitutionality of post-*Furman* death penalty statutes in Florida, Texas, North Carolina, and Louisiana (*Proffitt v. Florida; Jurek v. Texas; Woodson v. North Carolina;* and *Roberts v. Louisiana*). In *Proffitt* and *Jurek* the Court found that the death penalty statutes in Florida and Texas provided the procedural safeguards similar to the Georgia death penalty statute. In *Woodson* and *Roberts*, the Court invalidated the statutes in North Carolina and Louisiana because both states had incorporated a mandatory death penalty for anyone convicted of first degree murder or felony murder. As Justice Stewart stated in *Woodson*, the mandatory sentencing procedure did not allow for specific "consideration of relevant aspects of the character and record of each convicted defendant before the imposition upon him of a sentence of death. We believe that in capital cases the fundamental respect for humanity underlying the Eight Amendment . . . requires consideration of the character and record of the individual offender and the circumstances of the particular offense as a constitutionally indispensable part of the process of inflicting the penalty of death" (*Woodson*).

Continuing with the concept of individualized sentencing, the Court ruled in *Lockett v. Ohio* that each capital defendant is entitled to an individualized sentencing hearing. In that hearing, all relevant mitigating evidence and testimony should be admitted that might assist the jury in their task. The *Lockett* decision greatly expanded the role of mitigation. As a result, mitigation has evolved into a complete and thorough psychosocial history investigation and evaluation. Subsequently, the Court ruled that attorneys have an obligation to do a thorough mitigation investigation or a defendant's constitutional right to effective assistance of counsel would be violated (*Williams v. Taylor*). Recently, the Court reaffirmed the responsibility of the attorneys to perform a thorough mitigation investigation and that failure to do so would constitute ineffective assistance (*Wiggins v. Smith*).

In several cases, the Court ruled that executions should be prohibited, or at least delayed. In *Ford v. Wainwright*, the Supreme Court held that the Eighth Amendment prohibits execution of the insane — a term never clearly differentiated in this ruling from competency. The Court stated that the insane should not be executed, because such an execution has questionable retributive value, because there is no deterrent effect on people who cannot understand the reason for their execution and the full implication of the penalty, and because they are unable to assist in their own defense. Finally, the Court declared that executing insane defendants offends humanity. Yet executions could proceed if the defendant's mental state were restored.

In *Thompson v. Oklahoma*, the Court held that executing a criminal defendant who was under the age of 16 years old at the time of the offense constitutes cruel and unusual punishment in violation of the Eighth and Fourteenth Amendments. At that time 18 states explicitly established in their death penalty statutes that the defendant must be at least 16 years old at the time of the offense. Yet the Court also ruled in *Stanford v. Kentucky* that states could execute defendants who were 16 at the time of the offense.

For a period of time it appeared that the Court was indeed narrowing the class of individuals who might be eligible for execution. However, in 1989, the Supreme Court took up the question of mental retardation. In *Penry v. Lynaugh*, the Court refused to find that executing a mentally retarded person was a *per se* violation of the cruel and unusual punishment clause of the Eighth Amendment. Instead, the Court held that the Eighth Amendment did not necessarily preclude the execution of all mentally retarded persons simply by virtue of disability. The Court did state, however, that the jury is entitled to instructions as to the mitigating effect of mental retardation. The Court reasoned that, so long as mitigating circumstances are considered by the jury or judge, "an individualized determination whether 'death is the appropriate punishment' can be made in each particular case." The issue of mental retardation was finally decided in June of 2002 with the *Atkins* decision. The Court held that executing those with mental retardation violates the Eighth Amendment's ban on cruel and unusual punishment.

CASE LAW SUMMARIES

The Supreme Court cases included in this chapter have been selected and edited either for their historical importance and/or relevancy for the death penalty or for their impact in the practice of forensic psychology or psychiatry. These opinions, because they are relatively permanent, form the historical and legal doctrines upon which capital litigation rests. The opinions are listed by category for convenience. In some cases, the original fact patterns are presented in part to give perspective on the opinion. With the exception of *Booth v. Maryland* and

Penry v. Lynaugh, the following opinions, as of this writing, are the current law.

Constitutionality of the Death Penalty

Furman v. Georgia
408 U.S. 238 (1972)

William Henry Furman, a 26-year-old African American with a sixth grade education, was attempting to break into a home when he was discovered by the tenant. Furman shot and killed the tenant through a closed door. Furman was charged with murder. His case was decided in conjunction with two companion cases, *Jackson v. Georgia* and *Branch v. Texas*. In those cases the defendants, also African Americans, were charged with rape.

In the 5-4 decision, all nine justices filed separate opinions with the majority concluding, though for very different reasons, that the imposition and carrying out of the death sentence in the present cases constituted cruel and unusual punishment, in violation of the Eighth and Fourteenth Amendments. The following are brief excerpts from those opinions:

> Justice Douglas stated, "In a nation committed to equal protection of the laws there is no permissible 'caste' system of law enforcement. Yet we know that the discretion of judges and juries in imposing the death penalty enables the penalty to be selectively applied, feeding prejudices against the defendant if he is poor and despised, poor and lacking political clout, or if he is a member of a suspect or unpopular minority, and saving those who by social position may be in a more protected position."

> Justice Brennan stated, "In sum, the punishment of death is inconsistent with . . . four principles: Death is an unusually severe and degrading punishment; there is a strong probability that it is inflicted arbitrarily; its rejection by contemporary society is virtually total; and there is no reason to believe that it serves any penal purpose more effectively than the less severe punishment of imprisonment. The function of these principles is to enable a court to determine whether a punishment comports with human dignity. Death, quite simply, does not."

> Justice Stewart stated that these sentences are "cruel and unusual in the same way that being struck by lightening is cruel and unusual. . . . The petitioners were among a capriciously selected random handful

upon whom the sentence of death was imposed. . . . I simply conclude that the Eighth and Fourteenth Amendments could not tolerate the infliction of a sentence of death under legal systems which permitted this unique penalty to be so wantonly and so freakishly imposed."

Justice White stated, "But when imposition of the death penalty reached a certain degree of infrequency, it would be doubtful that any existing general need for retribution would be measurably satisfied. Nor could it be said with confidence that society's need for specific deterrence justifies death for so few when for so many in like circumstances life imprisonment, or shorter prison terms are judged sufficient, or that community values are measurably reinforced by authorizing a penalty so rarely invoked."

Justice Marshall stated, "We achieve a major milestone in the long road up from barbarism and join the approximately 70 other jurisdictions in the world which celebrate their regard for civilization and humanity by shunning capital punishment."

Justices Burger, Blackmun, Powell, and Rehnquist dissented, stating that the constitutional prohibition against cruel and unusual punishments could not be construed to bar the imposition of the punishment of death.

As a result of *Furman,* all death sentences were vacated and all former death row inmates were resentenced (without death) according to the state sentencing guidelines. None of these inmates could be resentenced to death for their previous crimes.

Gregg v. Georgia
428 U.S. 155 (1976)

After the United States Supreme Court's decision in *Furman* (see above), the Georgia legislature amended its statutory scheme. Under the new statutory provisions regarding imposition of the death penalty, guilt or innocence would be determined, either by a jury or the trial judge, in the first stage of a bifurcated trial. At least 1 of 10 aggravating circumstances specified in the statute must be found to exist beyond a reasonable doubt. In the second stage of the trial, mitigation arguments (as well as the findings from a presentence evaluation) would be presented either to the jury or to the trial judge. If the jury or trial judge returned a verdict of death, there would be an automatic appeal of the death sentence to determine if the sentence was imposed "under the influence of passion, prejudice, or any other arbitrary factor, whether the evidence supported the finding of a statutory aggravating circumstance, and whether the death sentence was excessive or disproportionate to the penalty imposed in similar cases, considering both the crime and the defendant."

Troy Gregg was convicted of two counts of armed robbery and two counts of murder, and the jury, after the penalty hearing in the bifurcated procedure, returned a sentence of death on each count. Gregg was found guilty not only of the murder but also of the statutory aggravating condition: armed robbery.

On certiorari, the United States Supreme Court affirmed and concluded that the imposition of the death penalty for the crime of murder under the Georgia statutes did not violate the prohibition against the infliction of cruel and unusual punishment under the Eighth and Fourteenth Amendments. The concerns expressed in *Furman* that the death penalty not be imposed in an arbitrary or capricious manner could be met by a carefully drafted statute ensuring that the sentencing authority was given adequate guidance and information for determining the appropriate sentence, a bifurcated sentencing proceeding being preferable as a general proposition.

The Court expressed the view that the death penalty did not, under all circumstances, constitute cruel and unusual punishment since the Eighth Amendment was not to be regarded as a static concept but was to draw its meaning from the evolving standards of decency that marked the progress of a maturing society. In addition the Court stated that

1. Although public perceptions of standards of decency were not conclusive — the Eighth Amendment requiring that punishment must accord with the dignity of man and not be excessive either as to its form or severity — nevertheless a legislature was not required to select the least severe penalty possible, so long as the penalty selected was not cruelly inhumane or disproportionate to the crime involved, and a heavy burden rested on those attacking the judgment of the representatives of the people,

2. at the time the Constitution and its amendments were adopted, capital punishment was accepted as a common sanction, and the Supreme Court, for nearly 200 years, had repeatedly recognized that capital punishment was not invalid per se,

3. after the decision in the *Furman* case, at least 35 states enacted new statutes providing for the death penalty for certain crimes, thus indicating society's endorsement of the death penalty,

4. retribution and deterrence, as social purposes served by the death penalty, were matters that could properly be considered by legislatures in terms of their own local conditions, and

5. capital punishment for murder could not be said to be invariably disproportionate to the crime, but instead was an extreme sanction, suitable to the most extreme of crimes." [Edited]

As a result of this decision, virtually all capital cases must (a) narrow the scope of death-eligible crimes, (b) allow for mitigation, and (c) provide an automatic appeal to the Supreme Court.

Coker v. Georgia
433 U.S. 584 (1977)

Ehrlich Coker was convicted of rape and sentenced to death by a jury. The Georgia Supreme Court affirmed both the conviction and sentence, and the court granted petitioner's writ of certiorari for the limited purpose of determining whether a death sentence for a rape conviction violated the Eighth Amendment. After conducting an examination of recent death penalty cases that invoked the Eighth Amendment, as well as the trend of state legislatures to pass or repeal laws concerning death sentences for persons convicted of rape, the U.S. Supreme Court held that a sentence of death was grossly disproportionate and excessive punishment for the crime of rape. Imposition of the death penalty for rape cases was cruel and unusual punishment and violated the Eighth Amendment.

Testimony on Future Dangerousness

Jurek v. Texas
428 U.S. 262 (1976)

Under the revised Texas statutes,

(1) Capital homicides were limited to intentional and knowing murders committed in the five specified situations of murder of a peace officer or fireman; murder committed in the course of kidnapping, burglary, robbery, forcible rape, or arson; murder committed while escaping or attempting to escape from a penal institution; murder committed for remuneration; and murder committed by a prison inmate when the victim is a prison employee.

(2) If a defendant were convicted of a capital offense, a separate resentence hearing must be held before the jury, where any relevant evidence may be introduced and arguments may be presented for or against the death sentence.

(3) The jury must answer the questions (a) whether the defendant's conduct that caused the death was committed deliberately and with the reasonable expectation that the death of the deceased or another would result, (b) whether there is a probability that the defendant would commit criminal acts of violence that would constitute a continuing threat to society, and (c) if raised by the evidence, whether the defendant's conduct in killing the deceased was unreasonable in response to the provocation, if any, by the deceased.

(4) If the jury finds that the state has proved beyond a reasonable doubt that the answer to each of the pertinent questions is yes, then the death sentence is imposed, but if the jury finds that the answer to any question is no, then a sentence of life imprisonment results.

(5) Death sentences are given expedited review on appeal.

Jerry Lane Jurek was convicted by a jury of murder for the killing of a 10-year-old girl by choking, strangling, and drowning her in the course of kidnapping and forcible rape. At a separate sentencing hearing, the jury then considered the two relevant statutory questions regarding aggravating and mitigating circumstances. The jury answered both questions with a unanimous "yes," and in accordance with the statute, the judge sentenced petitioner to death. On certiorari, the United States Supreme Court affirmed.

Barefoot v. Estelle
463 U.S. 880 (1983)

Thomas Barefoot was convicted of capital murder in a Texas court. He was subsequently sentenced to death after a separate sentencing hearing before the same jury that had convicted him. One of the questions the jury affirmed, as required for the death sentence to be imposed, was whether "there is a probability that the defendant would constitute a continuing threat to society." The state of Texas introduced into evidence on this question the defendant's prior convictions and his reputation for lawlessness. The state also called two psychiatrists, who in response to hypothetical questions, testified that the defendant would probably commit further acts of violence and represent a continuing threat to society. On appeal to the Texas Court of Criminal Appeals (and eventually to the United States Supreme Court), Barefoot's attorneys argued that the use of predictions of future behavior made by psychiatrists at the punishment hearing was unconstitutional because psychiatrists are not competent to predict future dangerousness and, therefore, that these predictions are so likely to produce erroneous sentences that their use violated the Eighth and Fourteenth Amendments of the United States Constitution. The attorneys also argued that allowing psychiatrists who had not personally examined the defendant to answer hypothetical questions was constitutional error.

On certiorari, the United States Supreme Court affirmed the judgment of the District Court. It was held that

> (1) the Constitution of the United States did not require that the defendant's death sentence be set aside on the ground that the testimony of the two psychiatrists should not have been allowed, since there was no showing that such testimony regarding the defendant's future dangerousness is almost entirely unreliable and that the factfinder and adversary system are not competent to uncover, recognize and take due account of the testimony's shortcomings, it is proper to base such testimony on hypothetical questions and without the psychiatrists' personal examination of the defendant, there being no constitutional barrier to applying the ordinary rules of evidence governing expert testimony, and there was no due process violation at the hearing on the basis that the doctors were permitted to give an opinion on the ultimate issue before the jury, that the hypothetical questions referred to controverted facts, and that the answers to the questions were so positive so as to be assertions of fact and not opinion, and (2) the Court of Appeals correctly denied the stay of execution pending appeal on the habeas corpus judgment, since although the court did not formally affirm the District Court's judgment, it did rule on the merits of the appeal, giving careful consideration to the primary issue. The court rejected the defendant's argument that expert testimony as to future dangerousness be disallowed in capital proceedings. The court acknowledges the American Psychiatric Association's opinion against having psychiatrists render such opinions, but declines to convert that opinion to the level of constitutional rules.

Therefore, psychiatric (or psychological) testimony regarding future dangerousness is admissible at sentencing hearing at capital trial.

Estelle v. Smith
451 U.S. 454 (1981)

On December 28, 1973, Ernest Benjamin Smith participated in an armed robbery of a grocery store during which a clerk was fatally shot by Smith's accomplice. Smith was indicted for capital murder in the state of Texas. The state trial court ordered that the defendant undergo a psychiatric examination to determine his competency to stand trial. After the psychiatrist concluded that he was competent, the defendant was tried by a jury and convicted. State law then required a separate penalty proceeding at which the jury had to assess the defendant's future dangerousness, one of three questions on which the state had the burden of proof beyond a reasonable doubt before the death sentence could be imposed. At the defendant's sentencing hearing, the state called as a witness the psychiatrist who had conducted the pretrial psychiatric examination. He testified that, among other things, the defendant was "going to go ahead and commit other similar or same criminal acts if given the opportunity to do so." The jury answered the three requisite questions in the affirmative, and the mandatory death penalty was imposed.

On certiorari, the United States Supreme Court held that the admission of the psychiatrist's testimony violated the defendant's Fifth Amendment privilege against compelled self-incrimination because the defendant was not advised before the pretrial examination that he had a right to remain silent and that any statement he made could be used against him at the sentencing proceeding. The defendant's statements to the psychiatrist were not given freely and voluntarily. [The admission of the psychiatrist's testimony violated the defendant's Sixth Amendment right to the assistance of counsel because defense counsel were not notified in advance that the psychiatric examination would encompass the issue of their client's future dangerousness, and therefore the defendant was denied the assistance of his attorneys in making the significant decision of whether to submit to the examination and to what end the psychiatrist's findings could be employed.] The Sixth Amendment right attaching when the doctor examined the defendant in jail and that interview proved to be a "critical stage" of the aggregate proceedings against the defendant.

As a practical matter, mental health experts should not undertake evaluations on capital defendants who are not represented by counsel and without counsel having been informed of the evaluation. The evaluation should be specific to the referral question (i.e., competency to stand trial) and not extend into other areas (i.e., criminal responsibility, mitigation). The defendant must normally be Mirandized according to state and federal law and informed that the information obtained may be used at sentencing and could be used to support a recommendation of death. However, in some jurisdictions, information gained as a part of a competency evaluation is not to be used for any other purpose. In defense-retained evaluations the assessment is within attorney-client privilege unless waived. As a point of information, the defendant may not have a right to have the attorney present during the evaluation.

Appointment of Mental Health Experts

Ake v. Oklahoma
470 U.S. 68 (1985)

Late in 1979, Glen Burton Ake was arrested and charged with murdering a couple and wounding their two children. His behavior at arraignment, and in other prearraignment incidents at the jail, was so bizarre that the trial judge, *sua sponte*, ordered him to be examined by a psychiatrist "for the purpose of advising with the Court as to his impressions of whether the Defendant may need an extended period of mental observation." The examining psychiatrist reported, "At times [Ake] appears to be frankly delusional. He claimed to be the 'sword of vengeance' of the Lord and that he would sit at the left hand of God in heaven." He diagnosed Ake as a probable paranoid schizophrenic and recommended a prolonged psychiatric evaluation to determine whether Ake was competent to stand trial. At a pretrial conference, the defense counsel informed the Court that the defendant would raise an insanity defense and asked the Court to arrange to have a psychiatrist perform an examination or to provide funds to allow the defense to arrange one because no inquiry had been made into the defendant's sanity at the time of the offense. The trial judge denied the motion. At the guilt phase, the sole defense was insanity, but there was no expert testimony for either side on the issue of the defendant's sanity at the time of the offense. The jury convicted the defendant on all counts. At the capital sentencing phase, the defendant had no expert witness to rebut the prosecution's testimony as to his future dangerousness, an aggravating factor, and the jury sentenced him to death. The Oklahoma Court of Criminal Appeals affirmed, holding that the defendant was not entitled to the services of a Court-appointed psychiatrist.

On certiorari, the United States Supreme Court reversed and remanded, basing their decision on the Fourteenth Amendment's due process clause. It was held "(1) that when a defendant in a criminal prosecution makes a preliminary showing that his sanity at the time of the offense is likely to be a significant factor at trial the Constitution requires that the state provide the defendant access to a psychiatrist if the defendant cannot otherwise afford one; (2) that a defendant is similarly entitled to the assistance of a psychiatrist at a capital sentencing proceeding at which the state presents psychiatric evidence of the defendant's future dangerousness; and (3) that under the facts presented, the defendant's sanity was a significant factor at both the guilt and sentencing phases and that the denial of psychiatric assistance constituted a deprivation of due process."

Though the opinion is specific in the appointment of a psychiatrist, most courts extend the opinion to include psychologists and other forensic experts. Usually the attorney will prepare a motion citing the qualifications of the expert and why the appointment is relevant.

Mitigating Circumstances

Lockett v. Ohio
438 U.S. 586 (1978)

Sandra Lockett was convicted of aggravated murder and sentenced to death in connection with a robbery-murder committed while she waited in the driver's seat of the getaway car. The State Supreme Court affirmed her conviction and sentence. On her petition for further review, the Supreme Court reversed the death sentence, holding that the Ohio death penalty statute violated the Eighth and Fourteenth Amendment prohibitions against cruel and unusual punishment because it did not permit the sentencer to consider a necessary range of mitigating factors, including Lockett's character, age, record, or the circumstances of the offense. The state statute was unconstitutionally narrow where it imposed a mandatory death sentence based on a finding that the victim did not induce the offense, that the defendant did not act under duress or coercion, and that the crime was not the product of the victim's mental deficiency. The Court could not consider, as constitutionally required, that defendant had not intended to kill the victim and that she played a minor role in the crime.

The Court reversed the judgment as to the death penalty and remanded for further proceedings, stating, "We are now faced with those questions and we conclude that the Eighth and Fourteenth Amendments require that the sentencer, in all but the rarest kind of capital case, not be precluded from considering, as a mitigating factor, any aspect of a defendant's character or record and any of the circumstances of the offense that the defendant proffers as a basis for a sentence less than death. We recognize that, in noncapital cases, the established practice of individualized sentences rests not on constitutional commands, but on public policy enacted into statutes. The considerations that account for the wide acceptance of individualization of sentences in noncapital cases surely cannot be thought less important in capital cases. Given that the imposition of death by public authority is so profoundly different from all other penalties, we cannot avoid the conclusion that an individualized decision is essential in capital cases. The need for treating each defendant in a capital case with that degree of respect due the uniqueness of the individual is far more important than in noncapital cases."

The *Lockett* decision is the first to establish a constitutional basis for mitigation.

Eddings v. Oklahoma
455 U.S. 104 (1982)

Monty Lee Eddings was a 16-year-old who ran away from home with several younger companions. When a highway patrolman stopped their car, Eddings used a shotgun in the car to kill the officer as he approached. Ordered to stand trial as an adult, the 16-year-old youth was found guilty of murder in the first degree by the District Court of Creek County, Oklahoma. Oklahoma's death penalty statute provided that in the sentencing proceeding, evidence may be presented as to "any mitigating circumstances" or as to any certain enumerated aggravating circumstances. At the sentencing hearing, the state alleged three of the aggravating circumstances, and, in mitigation, Eddings' attorneys presented substantial evidence of a turbulent family history, of beatings by a harsh father, and of severe emotional disturbance. The trial judge found that the state had proved each of the three alleged aggravating circumstances beyond a reasonable doubt and considered Eddings' youth as a mitigating circumstance but found, as a matter of law, that he could not consider in mitigation the circumstances of Eddings' unhappy upbringing and emotional disturbance and sentenced him to death.

Following unsuccessful state appeals, the United States Supreme Court reversed in part and remanded. The Court ruled that the imposition of the sentence of death on the 16-year-old was done without the type of individualized consideration of mitigating factors required by the Eighth and Fourteenth Amendments in capital cases.

Of particular interest were the comments by Justice Powell: "Even the normal 16-year-old customarily lacks the maturity of an adult. In this case, Eddings was not a normal 16-year-old; he had been deprived of the care, concern, and paternal attention that children deserve. On the contrary, it is not disputed that he was a juvenile with serious emotional problems, and had been raised in a neglectful, sometimes even violent, family background. In addition, there was testimony that Eddings' mental and emotional development were at a level several years below his chronological age. All of this does not suggest an absence of responsibility for the crime of murder, deliberately committed in this case. Rather, it is to say that just as the chronological age of a minor is itself a relevant mitigating factor of great weight, so must the background and mental and emotional development of a youthful defendant be duly considered in sentencing."

Like the *Lockett* decision *Eddings* establishes that there should be no state limitations on mitigating circumstances or evidence.

Skipper v. South Carolina
476 U.S. 1 (1986)

Ronald Skipper was convicted in a South Carolina trial court of capital murder and rape. The state sought the death penalty, and a separate sentencing hearing was held before the trial jury. In the course of that hearing, Skipper and his wife were allowed to testify that he had conducted himself well during the time he had spent in jail between his arrest and trial. The trial court excluded similar testimony by two of Skipper's jailers and a regular visitor, holding that such evidence was irrelevant and thus inadmissible under state precedents. He was sentenced to death. On appeal, Skipper's attorneys contended that the trial court had committed constitutional error by excluding relevant mitigating evidence.

On certiorari, the United States Supreme Court reversed as to the imposition of the death sentence and remanded for further proceedings. In the opinion, the Court stated "(1) that an adjustment to life in prison is an aspect of his character that is by its nature relevant to the sentencing determination in capital cases, and (2) that the exclusion of the jailers' and visitor's testimony as to the defendant's conduct in jail, which had not been offered as lay opinions regarding future behavior, had not been excluded solely as irrelevant evidence of future behavior, and was not merely cumulative of the less disinterested testimony of the defendant and his wife, therefore rendered the resulting death sentence invalid under the cruel and unusual punishment clause of the Eighth Amendment."

Exclusion of evidence that Skipper had adjusted well to incarceration between arrest and trial violates *Lockett*. The penalty phase judge's failure to admit evidence of Skipper's probable favorable adjustment to prison if his life was spared was harmful error, and therefore the death sentence was vacated. As a result of *Skipper* it is important, therefore, to collect all institutional records, including jail records, in order to assess the defendant's past adjustment as well as his or her likely adjustment to future incarceration. There is always the possibility, however, that such records may reveal information (such as previous incarcerations) that had been kept from jurors. Ultimately it would be the attorney's decision to weigh the pros and cons of introducing such evidence.

Juveniles and the Death Penalty*

Stanford v. Kentucky
492 U.S. 361 (1989)

See also
State v. Wilkins
736 S.W.2d 409 (1987)

Two cases addressed whether the imposition of capital punishment on juvenile offenders constituted cruel and unusual punishment prohibited by the Federal Constitution's Eighth Amendment. In one case, Kevin Stanford, who was then approximately 17 years and 4 months old, robbed a gas station, raped and sodomized a station attendant, and finally shot the attendant to death so that she could not identify him. He was convicted of murder, first degree sodomy, first degree robbery, and receiving stolen property and was sentenced to death plus 45 years of imprisonment. The Supreme Court of Kentucky, in affirming the conviction and sentence, (a) rejected the boy's contention that he had a constitutional right to treatment, (b) ruled that the District Court had not erred in certifying the boy for trial as an adult, and (c) stated that the boy's age and the possibility of rehabilitation were mitigating factors properly left to the consideration of the jury. In the second case, a boy who was then approximately 16 years and 6 months old conceived a plan to rob a convenience store — a plan that involved murdering whoever was behind the counter so as to leave no witness — and, in executing that plan, repeatedly stabbed the store's owner/operator and left her to die. A Missouri juvenile court certified the boy for trial as an adult, based on the viciousness of the crime, the boy's maturity, and the failure of the juvenile justice system to rehabilitate him after previous delinquent acts. The boy was then charged with first degree murder, armed criminal action, and carrying a concealed weapon, to which charges he pleaded guilty after a Missouri trial court found him competent and failed to dissuade him from waiving his rights. At a punishment hearing, (a) both the prosecution and the boy urged imposition of the death sentence, (b) expert witnesses testified that the boy had personality disorders but was aware of his actions and could distinguish right from wrong, and (c) the trial court found that the death penalty was appropriate, given the heinousness of the crime and the fact that it was committed in the course of a robbery. In affirming the boy's conviction and sentence, the Supreme Court of Missouri rejected arguments that the death sentence was disproportionate to the penalty imposed in other similar cases.

---

*When this book went to press, constitutionality was under review by the U.S. Supreme Court.

On certiorari, the United States Supreme Court affirmed. Although unable to agree on an opinion as to all of the factors to be considered in determining whether the imposition of capital punishment on an individual for a crime committed at 16 or 17 years of age constituted cruel and unusual punishment under the Eighth Amendment, five members of the Court agreed that there is no consensus forbidding the imposition of capital punishment on any person who murders at 16 or 17 years of age and that the death sentences in the cases at hand were valid.

Thompson v. Oklahoma
487 U.S. 815 (1988)

William Wayne Thompson, a 15-year-old boy, participated in the brutal murder of his brother-in-law, who had been abusing the boy's sister. The boy was a "child" for purposes of Oklahoma criminal law, but the prosecutor sought an order allowing the boy to be tried as an adult, pursuant to an Oklahoma statute which allows such a trial if "(1) the prosecution shows the prosecutive merit of the case, and (2) the court finds that there are no reasonable prospects for rehabilitation of the child within the juvenile system." An Oklahoma District Court, having heard psychiatric testimony and evidence of the boy's past violent behavior, granted such an order, and the boy was tried as an adult in the District Court of Grady County, Oklahoma. The boy was convicted of first degree murder and sentenced to death following the argument of the prosecutor at the sentencing hearing that the crime was "especially heinous, atrocious, or cruel" within the terms of a statutory aggravating circumstance. In affirming the boy's conviction and sentence, the Oklahoma Court of Criminal Appeals held that "(1) a minor who has been certified to stand trial as an adult may be punished as an adult, including a death sentence, without violating the cruel and unusual punishment clause of the Eighth Amendment to the Federal Constitution or similar provisions of the state constitution, and (2) the admission of two of the aforementioned photographs in the guilt phase of the trial — but not the sentencing phase — was improper because their prejudicial effect outweighed their probative value, but was harmless error because of the overwhelming evidence of the boy's guilt."

On certiorari, the United States Supreme Court vacated the judgment of the Court of Criminal Appeals and remanded the case with instructions to vacate the boy's death sentence. Although unable to agree on an opinion, five members of the Court agreed that the imposition of the death penalty against this defendant would violate the cruel and unusual punishment clause of the Eighth Amendment because of the boy's age at the time of his offense. "Less culpability should attach to a crime committed by a juvenile than to a comparable crime committed by an adult."

As a result of *Stanford* and *Thompson*, the Court has established that states cannot pursue the death penalty of defendants who were younger than 16 years of age at the time of the capital offense.

Mental Retardation

Penry v. Lynaugh
492 U.S. 302 (1989)

On the morning of October 25, 1979, Pamela Carpenter was brutally raped, beaten, and stabbed with a pair of scissors in her home in Livingston, Texas. She died a few hours later in the course of emergency treatment. Before she died, she described her assailant. Her description led two local sheriff's deputies to suspect Johnny Paul Penry, who had recently been released on parole after conviction on another rape charge. Penry subsequently gave two statements confessing to the crime and was charged with capital murder.

At a competency hearing held before trial, a clinical psychologist testified that Penry was mentally retarded with an IQ of 54. As a child, Penry was diagnosed as having organic brain damage, probably caused by trauma to the brain at birth. Penry was tested over the years as having an IQ between 50 and 63. The psychologist's evaluation also revealed that Penry, who was 22 years old at the time of the crime, had the mental age of a 6-1/2 year old, which means that "he has the ability to learn and the learning or the knowledge of the average 6-1/2 year old kid." Penry's social maturity, or ability to function in the world, was that of a 9 or 10 year old. The psychologist testified that "there's a point at which anyone with [Penry's] IQ is always incompetent, but, you know, this man is more in the borderline range."

In the Texas state court, even though the defendant presented evidence of his mental retardation and his background of childhood abuse, the jury (a) found the defendant competent to stand trial, and (b) at the guilt phase of the trial, rejected the insanity defense and found the defendant guilty of capital murder. Then, in the penalty phase of the trial and following the instructions from *Jurek*, the jury decided that death should be imposed on the defendant.

The Supreme Court ruled that a death sentence for a mentally retarded defendant is not categorically prohibited by the Eighth Amendment, but the defendant is entitled to instructions as to mitigating effect of mental retardation and childhood abuse. The Supreme Court remanded the matter for further proceedings so that a jury could consider Penry's mitigating circumstances (specifically his mental retardation) in determining whether to impose the death penalty.

Atkins v. Virginia
536 U.S. 304 (2002)

Daryl Renard Atkins was convicted of abduction, armed robbery, and capital murder and sentenced to death. At approximately midnight on August 16, 1996, Atkins and William Jones, armed with a semi-automatic handgun, abducted Eric Nesbitt, robbed him, drove him to an automated teller machine in his pickup truck where cameras recorded their withdrawal of additional cash, then took him to an isolated location where he was shot eight times and killed. Atkins was then convicted in a Virginia trial court on charges of abduction, armed robbery, and capital murder. At a second capital sentencing hearing — after an appellate ruling that the first hearing had used a misleading verdict form — the defense presented testimony by a forensic psychologist who said that the defendant was mildly mentally retarded, with an IQ of 59, while a prosecution expert witness expressed the view that the defendant was of at least average intelligence. A jury again sentenced Atkins to death.

On appeal, the Supreme Court of Virginia, in affirming the imposition of the death penalty in this instance, relied on the authority of *Penry v. Lynaugh* in rejecting the defendant's claim that because he allegedly was mentally retarded, he could not be sentenced to death.

On certiorari, the United States Supreme Court reversed and remanded. In its opinion, the Court stated that the execution of criminals who were mentally retarded was excessive and, thus, prohibited by the Eighth Amendment as cruel and unusual punishment. The Court based its argument on the following factors:

(1) Since the decision in *Penry v. Lynaugh*, a national consensus — with the consistency of the direction of change being more significant than the number of states — had developed against such executions, as evidenced by (a) the large number of states that had enacted prohibitions against such executions, (b) the absence of states reinstating the power to conduct such executions, and (c) the rarity of such executions even in states that allowed them.

(2) Evidence that such executions were opposed by religious and professional organizations and by the world community — and that polling data showed a widespread consensus among Americans against such executions — was not dispositive, but

lent further support to the conclusion that there was a consensus among those who had addressed the issue.

(3) In light of some deficiencies of persons who were mentally retarded with respect to information processing, communication, abstract and logical reasoning, impulse control, and understanding of others — which deficiencies diminished such persons' culpability — (a) it was questionable whether the death penalty's retribution and deterrence justifications were applicable to such offenders, and (b) such offenders faced a special risk of wrongful execution, due to their lesser ability to make a persuasive showing of mitigation.

In spite of the *Atkins* ruling, the issue of mental retardation was not entirely resolved. The Court left to the states the task of developing appropriate ways to identify and diagnose mentally retarded defendants or offenders. (See Chapter 10.)

Victim Impact

Booth v. Maryland
482 U.S. 496 (1987)

In 1983, Irvin Bronstein, 78, and his wife Rose, 75, were robbed and murdered in their West Baltimore home. The murderers, John Booth and Willie Reid, entered the Bronstein home to steal money for heroin. Booth, a neighbor of the Bronsteins, knew that the elderly couple could identify him. The victims were bound and gagged, and then stabbed repeatedly in the chest with a kitchen knife. The bodies were discovered 2 days later by the Bronsteins' son.

Booth was charged with two counts of first degree murder, and the jury found him guilty. During the sentencing phase the prosecutor was allowed to read to the jury a victim impact statement that included comments by family members of the victims on the character of the victims and their characterizations of the defendant and his crimes. The jury imposed the death penalty for one of the murders, and imposed life imprisonment for the other. On appeal, Booth's attorneys claimed that reading the victim impact statement to the jury violated the Eighth Amendment. The Court held that allowing the jury to consider the victim impact statement during the sentencing phase of defendant's capital murder trial violated the Eighth Amendment because (a) the information contained therein was irrelevant to the capital sentencing decision, and (b) the admission of the victim impact statement created a constitutionally unacceptable risk that the jury might impose the death penalty in an arbitrary and capricious manner.

Payne v. Tennessee
501 U.S. 808 (1991)

Pervis Tyrone Payne was convicted by a jury on two counts of first degree murder and one count of assault with intent to commit murder in the first degree. He was sentenced to death for each of the murders and to 30 years in prison for the assault. Payne argued that the statements of family members of the victims and remarks by the prosecutor during defendant's capital sentencing were highly prejudicial and contrary to the Supreme Court's holdings (see *Booth*) that such evidence was not admissible.

The Court affirmed the decision of the Tennessee Supreme Court, upholding the death sentence of defendant. The Court overruled its prior decisions in *Booth v. Maryland* and *South Carolina v. Gathers*, holding that evidence and argument relating to the victim and the impact of the victim's death on the victim's family were admissible at a capital sentencing hearing.

Therefore, victim impact testimony is permitted as long as it conforms to state law.

Jury Selection and Related Issues

Witherspoon v. Illinois
391 U.S. 510 (1968)

Removal of jurors merely because of general scruples against capital punishment denies due process right to an impartial jury. Jurors may be excluded for cause only if they make it "unmistakably clear" that they would automatically vote against the death penalty or that they could not be impartial as to guilt.

Wainwright v. Witt
469 U.S. 412 (1985)

The proper standard for determining when prospective jurors may be excluded for cause because of their views on capital punishment is whether the jurors' views would "prevent or substantially impair their performance of their duties as a juror in accordance with their instructions and their oath." In addition to dispensing with *Witherspoon*'s reference to "automatic" decision making, this standard does not require that a juror's bias be proved with "unmistakable clarity."

As a result of *Witt*, the criteria for removing jurors for cause based on their views on capital punishment was expanded.

Lockhart v. McCree
476 U.S. 162 (1986)

Despite the research on jury selection, the Supreme Court stated that removal for cause, from the jury that decides the guilt phase of a capital case, of persons whose attitudes toward capital punishment would prevent or substantially impair the performance of their duties does not violate the Sixth Amendment right to an impartial jury or to a jury drawn from a fair cross-section of the community.

"The court assumes (without accepting) the validity of the studies establishing that 'death qualification' produces juries which are somewhat more 'conviction prone' than 'non-death qualified' juries. Death qualifying jurors before the guilt phase of a capital trial does not offend constitutional rights to an impartial jury or a representative cross-section of the community seated as jurors."

Batson v. Kentucky
476 U.S. 79 (1986)

At trial, the prosecutor used his peremptory challenges to strike all four black persons on the venire and selected a jury composed only of white persons. The trial judge observed that the parties were entitled to use peremptory challenges to strike anyone for any reason. On appeal to the State Supreme Court, Batson's attorneys contended the facts established that prosecution had engaged in a systematic pattern of discriminatory challenges establishing an equal protection violation. The State Supreme Court affirmed the conviction. The Supreme Court reversed and remanded the case to the trial court, holding that "if the trial court decided the facts established *prima facie*, purposeful discrimination and the prosecution did not proffer a neutral explanation for its actions, petitioner's conviction must be reversed."

Morgan v. Illinois
504 U.S. 719 (1992)

Derrick Morgan was convicted of first degree murder and sentenced to death. On appeal, the Supreme Court found that Morgan was "entitled, upon his request, to inquiry discerning those jurors who, even prior to the state's case in chief, had predetermined the terminating issue of his trial, that being whether to impose the death penalty." The Court explained that any juror who stated that he or she would automatically vote for the death penalty without regard to the mitigating evidence would be announcing an intention not to follow the instructions to consider the mitigating evidence and to decide if it was sufficient to preclude imposition of the death penalty. Thus, during voir dire of the capital case, the Illinois trial court violated due process by refusing to ask potential jurors whether they would automatically impose the death penalty if the defendant were convicted.

Ring v. Arizona
536 U.S. 584 (2002)

In 1994, Timothy Ring was charged with murder, armed robbery, and related charges in the killing of the driver of a Wells Fargo armored van. The jury deadlocked on premeditated murder, but found Ring guilty of felony murder occurring in the course of the armed robbery. Under Arizona law, Ring could not be sentenced to death unless the judge determined that there were aggravating circumstances. In the *Ring* case, the judge (not the jury) found two aggravating circumstances as well as one nonstatutory mitigating circumstance (minimal criminal record) and sentenced Ring to death. In Arizona and several other states, judges, not juries, were determining whether aggravating factors existed and, therefore, whether to impose the death penalty. The Supreme Court ruled that allowing the sentencing judge, without a jury, to find aggravating circumstances necessary for imposition of the death penalty violates the right to a jury trial under the Sixth Amendment. Based on the Court's previous ruling in *Apprendi v. New Jersey*, the Constitution requires that any fact that increases the penalty for a crime beyond the prescribed statutory maximum must be determined by a jury. It is still unclear whether Ring will be retroactively applied to grant relief to capital defendants whose sentencing proceedings were in front of a judge or judge panel rather than a jury.

Race Discrimination
And the Death Penalty

McCleskey v. Kemp
481 U.S. 279 (1987)

In the Superior Court of Fulton County, Georgia, an African American defendant, Warren McCleskey, was convicted of murdering a white police officer during the course of a planned robbery. In order to consider the death penalty during the posttrial penalty hearing, the jury was required under Georgia law to find beyond a reasonable doubt that the murder was accompanied by one of the statutory aggravating circumstances. The jury found two such circumstances to have existed: (a) the commission of the murder during the course of an armed robbery, and (b) the fact that the victim was a peace officer engaged in the performance of his duties. The jury also considered the mitigating circumstances of the defendant's conduct although the defendant offered no mitigating evidence. The jury recommended that the defendant be sentenced to death, and the court followed the jury's recommendation. McCleskey's attorneys next filed a petition for a writ of habeas corpus in the United States District Court for the Northern District of Georgia, in which they claimed that the state's capital sentencing process was administered in a racially discriminatory manner in violation of the Eighth and Fourteenth Amendments. In support of the claim, the attorneys proffered a statistical study indicating that, even after taking account of numerous nonracial variables, defendants charged with killing whites were 4 times as likely to receive a death sentence in Georgia as defendants charged with killing blacks, and that black defendants were 11 times as likely to receive a death sentence as other defendants. The District Court dismissed the habeas corpus petition, holding that (a) the statistics did not demonstrate that the death penalty was imposed on the defendant in violation of the Eighth Amendment, and (b) the methodology of the study was flawed with respect to the Fourteenth Amendment claim. The United States Court of Appeals for the Eleventh Circuit affirmed, although it assumed the validity of the study itself.

On certiorari, the United States Supreme Court affirmed stating that "(1) the statistical evidence was insufficient to support an inference that any of the decision makers in accused's case acted with discriminatory purpose in violation of the equal protection clause of the Fourteenth Amendment, since (a) the accused offered no evidence of racial bias specific to his own case, and (b) the statistical evidence alone was not clear enough to prove discrimination in any one case, (2) the study was insufficient to prove that the state violated the equal protection clause by adopting the capital punishment statute and allowing it to remain in force despite its allegedly discriminatory application, and (3) the study was insufficient to prove that the state's capital punishment system was arbitrary and capricious in application and that therefore the accused's death sentence was excessive in violation of the Eighth Amendment."

Miller-El v. Cockrell
537 U.S. 322 (2003)

Thomas Miller-El, a Texas death row inmate, claimed that Dallas County prosecutors engaged in racially biased jury selection at the time of his trial in 1986. The Supreme Court ruled that Miller-El should have been given an opportunity to present evidence of racial bias during his federal appeal. The Court sent the case back to a lower court, where Miller-El would be granted a new hearing on his claims. Justice Kennedy wrote, "Irrespective of whether the evidence could prove sufficient to support a charge of systematic exclusion of African-Americans, it reveals that the culture of the district attorney's office in the past was suffused with bias against African-Americans in jury selections."

Competency to be Executed

Ford v. Wainwright
477 U.S. 399 (1986)

In a Florida state court, Alvin Ford was convicted of murder and sentenced to death. There was no suggestion that he was incompetent at the time of his offense, at trial, or at sentencing. Later, however, he began to manifest changes in behavior, indicating a mental disorder. At his attorneys' request, two psychiatrists examined him, concluding that Ford was not competent to "suffer" execution. Following specified state procedures, the governor of Florida appointed a panel of three psychiatrists to evaluate whether the defendant had the mental capacity to understand the nature of the death penalty and the reasons it was imposed on him. Though they differed on their diagnoses, they agreed that the defendant understood his situation and the nature of the death penalty. After several unsuccessful appeals the case was presented to the United States Supreme Court.

The Court reversed and remanded the case stating that the Eighth Amendment prohibits a state from carrying out the death sentence on a prisoner who is insane. In his concurring opinion, Justice Powell stated that the Eighth Amendment "forbids the execution only of those who are unaware of the punishment they are about to suffer and why they are to suffer it." The Court also found the Florida procedures for determining such an issue were defective, thus depriving the inmate of constitutional protections.

The Eighth Amendment bars execution of death row inmates who had become so "insane" that they no longer understood they were going to be put to death or the reason for their execution. In this context "insanity" refers to a prisoner's lack of understanding of the relationship between the crime and the possible punishment. Insanity, in this instance, does not refer to one's criminal culpability.

Competency to Plea

Godinez v. Moran
509 U.S. 389 (1993)

Richard Allen Moran was charged with three counts of first degree murder after shooting and killing three persons. Following an attempted suicide, he pleaded not guilty in a Nevada state court. Two court-appointed psychiatrists concluded that Moran was competent to stand trial. Two-and-a-half months after the evaluations, Moran informed the Court that he wished to discharge his attorneys and change his pleas to guilty. The Court accepted the waiver of counsel and the guilty pleas after "(1) finding, on the basis of the previous psychiatric reports, that the defendant (a) understood the nature of the charges against him, (b) was able to assist in his defense, (c) knew the consequences of entering a guilty plea, and (d) was able to waive the right of counsel knowingly and intelligently; and (2) determining, on questioning the defendant, that he (a) was knowingly and intelligently waiving his right to counsel, and (b) was freely and voluntarily pleading guilty." A sentencing panel of the Court sentenced the defendant to death for each of the murders, and the Supreme Court of Nevada affirmed with respect to two of the murders. Moran, claiming that he had been mentally incompetent to represent himself, sought postconviction relief in state court. After an evidentiary hearing, the state court rejected Moran's claim on the basis of the psychiatrists' findings of competency. After several unsuccessful appeals through the various courts, Moran's case was reversed and remanded in the United States Court of Appeals for the Ninth Circuit. The case was then appealed to the United States Supreme Court.

The Court reversed the Ninth Circuit's opinion stating that "(1) although the decision to plead guilty is a profound one, such a decision is no more complicated than the sum total of decisions that all criminal defendants, not merely those who plead guilty, may be called upon to make during the course of a trial; (2) if the rational-understanding standard is adequate for defendants who plead not guilty, that standard is necessarily adequate for those who plead guilty; (3) there is no reason to believe that the decision to waive counsel requires an appreciably higher level of mental functioning than the decision to waive other constitutional rights; and therefore (4) the standard for measuring a criminal defendant's competency to plead guilty or waive the right to counsel is not higher than, or different from, the rational-understanding competency standard for standing trial."

The result of this decision is that a finding of "competency to stand trial" presumes competency on all other related matters such as competency to enter a plea, competency to waive counsel, competency to waive a jury, or competency to waive further appeals. On the other hand, it could be assumed that if one were not competent in any of these areas, then the defendant would not be competent to stand trial. Consider, for example, the decision to waive a jury and have a case heard before a judge or a panel of judges. The defendant must understand that he or she would be giving up Sixth Amendment rights to a jury trial and all of the related aspects of jury selection and constitutional protections.

Forced Medication

Riggins v. Nevada   *Sell v. United States*
504 U.S. 127 (1992)   539 U.S. 166 (2003)

Following arrest, David Riggins was placed on an antipsychotic drug and found competent to stand trial although one psychiatrist testified that he was not competent. Riggins' attorneys filed a motion to be taken off drugs until after trial. The trial court denied the motion without explaining its rationale. He was convicted of murder and robbery, and the State Supreme Court affirmed his convictions. The Supreme Court reversed, holding that once a defendant filed a motion to terminate administration of antipsychotic medication, the state became obligated to establish the need for the drug and the medical appropriateness of the drug. The Court found that the trial court erred by allowing administration of the drug to continue without making any determination of the need for this drug or pursuing reasonable alternatives to forced medication. The Court also found that it was possible that the side effects of the medications would have an impact upon Riggins' outward appearance, the content of his testimony on direct or cross-examination, his ability to follow the proceedings, or the substance of his communication with counsel.

Therefore, the forced administration of antipsychotic medication (after a defendant was found competent to stand trial) violated rights guaranteed by the Sixth and Fourteenth Amendments. The administration of Mellaril was involuntary once Riggins' motion to terminate its use was denied which resulted in trial prejudice and no "essential state interest" to maintain medication existed. In *Sell*, the Court ruled that the Constitution permits the government to administer antipsychotic drugs involuntarily "to render a mentally ill defendant competent to stand trial on serious criminal charges if the treatment is medically appropriate, is substantially unlikely to have side effects that may undermine the trial's fairness, and, taking account of less intrusive alternatives, is necessary significantly to further important governmental trial-related interests."

Singleton v. Norris
124 S.Ct. 74 (2003), 319 F.3d 1018 (2003)

The Supreme Court refused to grant relief and therefore let stand *Singleton v. Norris,* the ruling permitting the state of Arkansas to forcibly medicate a mentally ill death row inmate in order for him to be executed. The Court found it in the state of Arkansas' best interest for Singleton to be forcibly treated and executed rather than left untreated but alive. (Charles Singleton was executed on January 6, 2004.)

Right to Counsel

Gideon v. Wainwright
372 U.S. 335 (1963)

Charged in a Florida state court with a noncapital felony, Clarence Earl Gideon appeared without funds (*informa pauperis* — in the manner of a pauper) and without counsel and asked the Court to appoint counsel for him. This was denied on the ground that the state law permitted appointment of counsel for indigent defendants in capital cases only. Gideon conducted his own defense "about as well as could be expected of a layman," and was convicted and sentenced to imprisonment. Subsequently, he applied to the State Supreme Court for a writ of habeas corpus, on the ground that his conviction violated his rights under the Federal Constitution. The State Supreme Court denied all relief.

The United States Supreme Court held that "the right of an indigent defendant in a criminal trial to have the assistance of counsel is a fundamental right essential to a fair trial, and petitioner's trial and conviction without the assistance of counsel violated the Fourteenth Amendment." Gideon overruled the 1942 case of *Betts v. Brady* where the Court said that counsel would be provided only in cases of "special circumstances" such as a questionable judiciary, or a defendant who was young, ignorant, or handicapped.

Right to Effective Counsel

Strickland v. Washington
466 U.S. 668 (1984)

During a 10-day period in September 1976, David Leroy Washington committed three murders which included stabbing, torture, kidnapping, assaults, attempted murders, attempted extortion, and theft. Washington pleaded guilty in a Florida trial court and told the trial judge that, although he had committed a string of burglaries, he had no significant prior criminal record and that at the time of his criminal spree he was under extreme stress caused by his inability to support his family. The trial judge told Washington that he had "a great deal of respect for people who are willing to step forward and admit their responsibility" and then sentenced him to death. Washington's attorney decided not to do any background investigation of his client nor did he request a psychiatric evaluation or presentence report. His decision was based, in part, to avoid cross-examination on various issues, including Washington's criminal history.

Washington's attorneys appealed claiming ineffective assistance at the sentencing proceeding in several respects, including his failure to request a psychiatric report, to investigate and present character witnesses, and to seek a presentence report.

After several unsuccessful state court appeals, the Federal Court of Appeals reversed the sentencing stating that the Sixth Amendment accorded criminal defendants a right to counsel rendering "reasonably effective assistance given the totality of the circumstances." The Supreme Court affirmed the Court of Appeals' decision, stating that "ineffective assistance of counsel entitling a defendant to a reversal of the guilt or sentencing phases is proven when counsel's performance is shown to be deficient in that it fell below an objective standard of reasonableness based on prevailing professional norms, and there is a reasonable probability that but for counsel's unprofessional errors, the result of the proceeding would have been different."

Williams v. Taylor
529 U.S. 362 (2000)

In a Virginia trial court, Terry Williams was convicted of robbery and capital murder. At his sentencing hearing, the jury heard from Williams' mother and two neighbors, all of whom testified that Williams was not violent. The jury also heard from a psychiatrist who testified that Williams had removed the bullets from his gun in the course of earlier robberies. Finally, defense counsel's closing was devoted to explaining that it was difficult to find a reason that the jury should spare Williams' life.

The mitigating evidence that trial counsel failed to present to the jury showed that Williams' parents had been imprisoned for the criminal neglect of Williams and his siblings, that Williams had been severely and repeatedly beaten by his father, that he had been committed to the custody of the social services bureau for 2 years during his parents' incarceration (including one stint in an abusive foster home), and then, after his parents were released from prison, had been returned to his parents' custody. The consequence of counsel's failure to conduct the requisite, diligent investigation into his client's troubling background and unique personal circumstances manifested itself during his generic, unapologetic closing argument, providing the jury with no reasons to spare Williams' life.

The Supreme Court ruled that "(1) Williams had been deprived of the constitutional right to the effective assistance of counsel, as defined in *Strickland v. Washington* (see above), and (2) the Virginia Supreme Court's refusal to set aside the death sentence was a decision that was contrary to or involved an unreasonable application of clearly established federal law, as determined by the United States Supreme Court."

Wiggins v. Smith
539 U.S. 510 (2003)

On September 17, 1988, police discovered a 77-year-old woman drowned in the bathtub of her ransacked apartment in Woodlawn, Maryland. Kevin Wiggins was convicted by a judge and then sentenced to death by a jury on October 18, 1989. On appeal Wiggins' attorneys argued that his trial counsel had been constitutionally defective by failing to investigate and present mitigating evidence. Had they done such an investigation, trial counsel would have found that Wiggins came from an extremely dysfunctional family noted by severe physical and sexual abuse suffered at the hands of his mother and while in the care of a series of foster parents. Much of the relevant information came from state social services, medical, and school records, as well as interviews with Wiggins and numerous family members. The investigating social worker chronicled Wiggins' bleak life history.

According to the social worker, Wiggins' mother was a chronic alcoholic who frequently left Wiggins and his siblings home alone for days, forcing them to beg for food and to eat paint chips and garbage. Mrs. Wiggins' abusive behavior included beating the children for breaking into the kitchen, which she often kept locked. She had sex with men while her children slept in the same bed and, on one occasion, forced Wiggins' hand against a hot stove burner resulting in his hospitalization. He was placed by the state in foster care and was physically abused, repeatedly molested, and raped by a foster father. At age 16, he ran away from his foster home and began living on the streets. He returned intermittently to additional foster homes and on more than one occasion was gang-raped. After leaving the foster care system, Wiggins entered a Job Corps program and was allegedly sexually abused by his supervisor. The jury was not presented with any of this information.

In their previous ruling, the Supreme Court stated in *Williams v. Taylor* (see above) that "counsel's failure to uncover and present voluminous mitigating evidence at sentencing could not be justified as a tactical decision." The Court's decision in this case was not whether counsel should have presented a mitigation case. Rather, the Court focused on whether the investigation supporting counsel's decision not to introduce mitigating evidence of Wiggins' background *was itself reasonable* (italics in original). In other words an attorney cannot make a strategic decision regarding whether to utilize mitigating information that he or she has not yet gathered and is therefore not yet known. The Court concluded that given both the nature and the extent of the abuse Wiggins suffered, there was a reasonable probability that a competent attorney, aware of this history, would have introduced it at sentencing in an admissible form. Justice O'Connor wrote, "Had the jury been able to place Wiggins' excruciating life history on the mitigating side of the scale, there is a reasonable probability that at least one juror would have struck a different balance." The case was remanded for re-sentencing.

Aiding and Abetting

Enmund v. Florida
458 U.S. 782 (1982)

On April 1, 1975, Sampson and Jeanette Armstrong had gone to the back door of the house of Thomas and Eunice Kersey (age 86 and 74) and asked for water for an overheated car. Evidence showed that Sampson Armstrong, and perhaps Jeanette, shot and killed both of the Kerseys, dragged them into the kitchen, took their money, and fled. Earl Enmund was a passenger in the car. The jury found both Enmund and Sampson Armstrong guilty of two counts of first degree murder and one count of robbery. At separate sentencing hearings the jury recommended the death penalty for both defendants in spite of the evidence that Enmund never intended to kill anyone.

On certiorari, the United States Supreme Court reversed and remanded stating that "the Eighth and Fourteenth Amendments were violated by the imposition of the death penalty on the defendant, who aided and abetted a felony in the course of which a murder was committed by others but who did not himself kill, attempt to kill, intend to kill, or contemplate that life would be taken."

Jury Instructions on
Life Without Parole

Kelly v. South Carolina   See also
534 U.S. 246 (2002)   *Simmons v. South Carolina*
                                              512 U.S. 154 (1994)

In 1996, William Arthur Kelly was indicted for murder and other crimes, and the defendant was convicted on all charges in a South Carolina trial court. During the trial's sentencing phase, the prosecutor (a) presented evidence that the defendant had made a knife while in prison and had taken part in an escape attempt with plans to hold a guard hostage; (b) elicited evidence of the defendant's sadism at an early age and his current desires to kill anyone who irritated him; (c) expressed the hope that the jurors would "never in their lives again have to experience . . . being some thirty feet away from such a person" as the defendant; and (d) spoke of the defendant, in the closing argument, as a "dangerous, bloody, butcher." Defense counsel requested the trial judge to instruct the jurors that the defendant would be ineligible for parole if sentenced to life imprisonment. The trial court denied the requested instruction on the ground that the state's evidence went to the defendant's character and characteristics rather than to future dangerousness. The jury found five statutory aggravating circumstances and returned a recommendation of death.

On certiorari, the United States Supreme Court reversed the South Carolina Supreme Court's judgment stating that "in the sentencing phase of a capital murder trial in South Carolina, the federal constitutional due process entitles the defendant, under circumstances presented, to jury instruction as to defendant's ineligibility for parole."

Mandatory Death Penalty

Roberts v. Louisiana
428 U.S. 325 (1976)

The defendant claimed that the imposition of the death penalty was cruel and unusual punishment in violation of the Eighth and Fourteenth Amendments based on jury instructions under Louisiana's Code of Criminal Procedure that did not allow the jury to consider the facts surrounding the murder and the defendant's character when assessing the death penalty. In essence, this was another example of a mandatory death penalty. The Court struck down the mandatory death penalty created by the Louisiana legislature.

Woodson v. North Carolina
428 U.S. 280 (1976)

The North Carolina statute making death penalty mandatory for first degree murder, which includes any willful, deliberate, and premeditated killing and any murder committed in perpetrating or attempting to perpetrate a felony was held to be unconstitutional.

Chapter 4

STAGES OF A CAPITAL CASE

One of the common complaints from supporters of the death penalty concerns the length of time between arrest and eventual execution. In 2002, 71 prisoners were executed with an average length of time spent on death row of 10 years and 7 months, 15 months less than for those executed in 2001 (Department of Justice, National Criminal Justice Reference Service [DOJ NCJ] 201848). By the end of 2003, 3,515 prisoners were on death row with California having the most (625), followed by Texas (453), and Florida (380) (Death Penalty Information Center statistics). Many appeals last well over 20 years. The lengthy time interval between conviction and execution and the associated appellate review occur to provide the higher standard of reliability called for under *Lockett*. As a result, between 1972 and 2002, 33% of death penalty convictions had been reduced to life sentences or overturned. The following provides a brief overview of the various stages of a capital case. Forensic evaluations may be requested at any of the stages.

In order to be eligible for the death penalty, a person must commit aggravated or first degree murder combined with one of the aggravating factors listed by the state or federal government. Treason is the only federal crime that could result in the death penalty without actually having committed a murder. Currently 38 states and the federal government permit capital punishment. In most jurisdictions, the prosecutor decides whether to charge a defendant with a capital crime. In summarizing the issues of capital punishment, Latzer (1998) states that each state legislature is free to adopt laws with regard to capital punishment as long as those laws are constitutional. A survey of death penalty statutes across the country demonstrates a wide range of death-eligible acts, with prosecutors having a considerable amount of discretion in determining whether to charge someone with a capital crime. So some progress has been made in restricting the range of offenses and rendering the process less arbitrary and capricious, but much inconsistency remains in determining whether to charge a defendant capitally.

Capital trials are bifurcated. The first phase determines the guilt or innocence of the defendant as to both the crime and the death penalty specifications (though many states defer the jury's consideration of aggravating factors until the penalty phase). If found guilty of death penalty specifications (statutory aggravating factors), there is a second trial (hearing) to determine the appropriate sentence. In most states, the same jury sits for both the first and second trial. Following testimony in the second phase of the trial, the jury recommends to the court the sentence — either the death penalty or a life sentence that is usually defined as "life without parole" or some very lengthy sentence (25 or 30 years) before the defendant is eligible for parole.

PRETRIAL

Following arrest and before trial, there are a number of intermediate steps taken in order to prepare a capital case. In the vast majority of capital cases, defendants are denied bond and waive "speedy trial" in order give their attorneys time to prepare. The following is the usual order of events prior to trial:

Arrest
Interrogation
Appointment of Counsel
Determination Whether to Set Bail (rarely granted in capital cases)
Notice of Intent to Seek Death Filed by Prosecutor
Discovery
Possible Competency Evaluation
Investigation
Motions for Experts Filed and Heard
Additional Motions (change of venue, etc.)
Hearing to Determine Competency
If Not Competent, Then Competency Restoration
Possible Evaluation for Criminal Responsibility
If Competent, Then Proceed to Trial

JURY SELECTION

In order to be selected in a capital case, a juror must be "death qualified." Jurors are questioned about death penalty attitudes to determine if their views would "prevent or substantially impair the performance of their duties as a juror in accordance with their instructions and their oath" (see *Wainwright v. Witt*). This permits both the prosecutor and defense attorneys to ask the court to remove a juror "for cause" or to use peremptory challenges — often limited to 12 or fewer depending on the jurisdiction. Jury selection in a capital case can take days or months depending on the jurisdiction, the leeway given by judges, and pretrial publicity.

If a defendant is found guilty and sentenced to death, he or she is entitled to an automatic appeal.

TRIAL

An indigent defendant has a Constitutional right for appointed counsel at trial (see *Gideon v. Wainwright*; *Johnson v. Zerbst*; and *Powell v. Alabama*). In most jurisdictions, two attorneys are appointed to indigent defendants charged with a death penalty crime. These attorneys may be appointed from the private sector or through the local or state office of the public defender.

As stated previously, there are two separate trials in a capital proceeding: one to determine guilt or innocence and one to determine the appropriate sentence. At the guilt/innocence phase, the trier of fact (i.e., the jury or panel of judges), determines whether the defendant is guilty of the offense. In addition to that finding, the jury must also determine if the defendant is guilty of one or more aggravating circumstances, thus initiating a sentencing hearing on the death penalty specifications. If the accused is acquitted or found guilty of a lesser, noncapital offense, the trial is concluded.

If the jury has found the accused guilty of one or more aggravating factors, a separate trial (hearing) convenes in order to hear testimony specific to mitigation and sentencing. At this stage, defense attorneys would put into evidence those factors they believe are relevant for the jury to consider. Mitigating factors defy definition, for they will most often be unique to the individual on trial. In a broad sense, they are factors about the circumstances of the offense itself, as well as the offender's character, background, and personal history, including, where applicable, his or her psychological profile. The defense must be afforded great leeway in presenting this evidence, and the jury is required to consider it:

> The eighth and fourteenth amendments require that the sentencer, in all but the rarest kind of capital case, not be precluded from considering, as a mitigating factor, any aspect of a defendant's character, or record and any of the circumstances of the offense that the defendant proffers as a basis for a sentence less than death. *Lockett v. Ohio*, 438 U.S. 586, 604 (1978)

> Just as the State may not by statute preclude the sentencer from considering any mitigating factor, neither may the sentencer refuse

to consider, as a matter of law, any relevant mitigating evidence. *Eddings v. Oklahoma,* 455 U.S. 104, 113-114 (1982)

After hearing and considering this evidence, the jury will determine whether the aggravating factors outweigh the mitigation. If the jury unanimously finds that the aggravation outweighs mitigation, it will be required to return a verdict calling for the death penalty. Otherwise, a form of a life prison sentence will be imposed. Jurors must be unanimous for death. In some jurisdictions, life is the automatic sentence when jurors cannot agree on death. Jurors need not state their reasons for a life sentence. In other states (e.g., California), if the jury is not unanimous (for life or death) then a mistrial is declared and another sentencing proceeding may occur.

DIRECT APPEAL

The stage of direct appeal looks for potential errors that occurred at trial and would have been known at trial based on transcripts (rulings on jury selection, admission of evidence, jury instructions, etc.). Indigent defendants still have a right to counsel (see Cunningham & Vigen, 1999 and *Douglas v. California*). This direct appeal stage proceeds through state appellate review and federal appellate review — though not necessarily reviewed by the U.S. Supreme Court.

APPLICATION FOR UNITED STATES SUPREME COURT REVIEW

Once the conviction and death sentence are upheld by the State Supreme Court, the defendant may file a petition for *certiorari* to the United States Supreme Court seeking to have the court find important, unresolved, constitutional issues and accept the case for review. In only a small portion of all capital convictions will the high court engage in this "direct review."

POSTCONVICTION PROCEEDINGS

Postconviction review (which can be at both the state and federal level) consists of an analysis of what is not on the record and may not have been known at the time of trial (e.g., prosecutorial misconduct, juror misconduct, ineffective assistance of counsel, newly discovered

DNA evidence, etc.). The postconviction process is, perhaps, the last resort in guarding against miscarriages of justice.

At the postconviction level, an indigent prisoner has no constitutional right to counsel, though counsel is usually provided through various resources including the state public defenders. Cunningham and Vigen (1999) discuss some of the legal issues with appointed counsel set forth under *Murray v. Giarratano*. The Court may stay an execution date in order to consider the petition. In many states, no execution date is set if the condemned person promptly files an application for postconviction relief.

A motion for postconviction relief consists of a review of the entire trial transcript and an analysis of what was done, what was not done, and what should have been done in preparing the case for trial. Often in preparing for postconviction, a psychological evaluation will be requested, and numerous records will be reviewed that may not have been available at trial. A common attack at this point in the review process is a claim of ineffective assistance of counsel. For example, many postconviction petitions often uncover a plethora of previous psychological evaluations on the defendant that were not obtained prior to trial. These records may have been relevant in laying the foundation for both trial and mitigation. Without such records, the defense attorney could not have made an informed decision regarding trial and mitigation strategy and the jury would not have a complete understanding of the defendant and any relevant information concerning his or her mental state. Had the jury been aware of the defendant's psychological functioning, then it may have not recommended the death penalty. The failure of counsel to investigate mitigation, the failure to object to certain evidence, and the failure to secure mental health experts all can be grounds for reversal at this stage.

Either side may appeal the decision and request review by the United States Supreme Court.

FEDERAL HABEAS CORPUS PROCEEDINGS

A person in custody following a state court conviction may petition for a writ of habeas corpus in the United States District Court on the grounds that the conviction or sentence under which he or she is being held was obtained in violation of the Constitution, laws, or treaties of the United States. This is a civil action brought against the warden of the prison where the person is being held or against the state commissioner of corrections. The District Court is not required to, but it may permit discovery and may hold an evidentiary hearing and take evidence. The federal courts will almost always issue a stay of execution until all habeas proceedings, including appeals, are concluded.

An appeal may be taken to the United States Court of Appeals. The indigent petitioner must obtain a certificate of probable cause to appeal showing the issues as debatable among jurists of reason. Either side can petition to the United States Supreme Court.

Under certain circumstances, a condemned person may seek state and federal review a second time, but only upon demonstrating sufficient reasons for failure to bring the issue or supporting evidence in the first postconviction appeal.

CASE EXAMPLE:
THE SLEEPING ATTORNEY

As an example of the appellate process, consider the case of Calvin Jerold Burdine (see *Burdine v. Johnson*). In 1984, he was convicted in Texas of aggravated murder following a trial that lasted a total of 12 hours and 51 minutes over 6 days. During that time, his attorney was reported to have been sleeping on at least 10 occasions and for up to 10 minutes at a time. Eight witnesses, including jurors and the clerk of courts, verified this. However, the issue of the sleeping attorney could not be raised on direct appeal because no one had placed it on the record at the trial in chief, and, therefore, it was not subject to review. In 1986, Burdine's direct appeals were denied. He was also denied review twice in 1987. (It is interesting to note that Burdine was represented by the same attorney both at trial and during the direct appeal.) His first habeas petition in June of 1994 was also denied.

Burdine filed a second state habeas application nearly 11 years after trial, claiming, for the first time, denial of assistance of counsel because his attorney repeatedly slept at trial. The state trial court conducted an evidentiary hearing in February 1995. That April, it recommended relief being granted, finding that Burdine's attorney did sleep during portions of the trial. The state trial court concluded that such conduct was "presumptively prejudicial."

The state appealed the trial court's decision to the Texas Court of Criminal Appeals. That court, though agreeing that the attorney had been sleeping, ruled against Burdine claiming that he was not entitled to relief because he had not demonstrated prejudice. In other words, Burdine had not proved that his sleeping attorney was ineffective based on the *Strickland* standard. Burdine could not prove that, while sleeping, his attorney failed to adequately represent him.

Following that decision, the state habeas court determined that defense counsel for Burdine was, in effect, absent during portions of the trial and therefore reversed the previous decision by the Texas State Court of Appeals. The decision of the Texas State Court of Appeals was then appealed to the United States District Court. Finally, District Court ruled in favor of Burdine stating that his "unconscious counsel equated to no counsel at all," and the case was reversed and remanded. The appeal on this seemingly obvious issue lasted 17 years. Burdine is now awaiting a new trial.

Chapter 5

AGGRAVATING AND MITIGATING FACTORS AND JURY INSTRUCTIONS

AGGRAVATING FACTORS

Following the *Furman v. Georgia* decision and as a result of *Gregg v. Georgia*, each state and the federal government had to narrow the class of individuals eligible for the death penalty, allow for individualized sentencing, and provide for appellate review. As was stated in *Furman*, current death penalty laws were unconstitutional in part because of the arbitrary and capricious nature of the process by which certain individuals were selected for capital punishment. Therefore, most state legislatures had to create death penalty laws which would satisfy the issues raised in *Furman* and *Gregg*. In most instances, murder, even if committed with prior calculation and design, would not be a death-eligible crime. The murder had to occur with at least one aggravating factor. State legislatures, therefore, outlined specific aggravating factors that, if presented, would make a murder a capital offense potentially punishable by death. The following is a list of typical legislative statutory factors that must be present for a capital offense.

Evidence to Be Considered in Assessing Punishment In First Degree Murder Cases for Which Death Penalty Was Authorized

Statutory Aggravating Circumstances for a Murder In the First Degree Offense Shall Be Limited to the Following:

1. The offense was committed by a person with a prior record of conviction for murder in the first degree, or the offense was

committed by a person who has one or more serious assaultive criminal convictions.

2. The murder in the first degree offense was committed while the offender was engaged in the commission or attempted commission of another unlawful homicide.

3. The offender by his or her act of murder in the first degree knowingly created a great risk of death to more than one person by means of a weapon or device which would normally be hazardous to the lives of more than one person.

4. The offender committed the offense of murder in the first degree for himself or herself or for another, in order to receive money or any other thing of monetary value from the victim of the murder or another.

5. The murder in the first degree was committed against a judicial officer, former judicial officer, prosecuting attorney or former prosecuting attorney, circuit attorney or former circuit attorney, assistant prosecuting attorney or former assistant prosecuting attorney, assistant circuit attorney or former assistant circuit attorney, peace officer or former peace officer, or elected official or former elected official during or because of the exercise of his or her official duty.

6. The offender caused or directed another to commit murder in the first degree or committed murder in the first degree as an agent or employee of another person.

7. The murder in the first degree was outrageously or wantonly vile, horrible, or inhuman in that it involved torture or depravity of mind.

8. The murder in the first degree was committed against any peace officer or fireman while engaged in the performance of his or her official duty.

9. The murder in the first degree was committed by a person in, or who has escaped from, the lawful custody of a peace officer or place of lawful confinement.

10. The murder in the first degree was committed for the purpose of avoiding, interfering with, or preventing a lawful arrest or custody in a place of lawful confinement of himself or herself or another.

11. The murder in the first degree was committed while the defendant was engaged in the perpetration or was aiding or encouraging another person to perpetrate or attempt to perpetrate a felony of any degree of rape, sodomy, burglary, robbery, kidnapping, or any felony offense.

12. The murdered individual was a witness or potential witness in any past or pending investigation or past or pending prosecution and was killed as a result of his or her status as a witness or potential witness.
13. The murdered individual was an employee of an institution or facility of the department of corrections of this state or local correction agency and was killed in the course of performing his or her official duties, or the murdered individual was an inmate of such institution or facility.
14. The murdered individual was killed as a result of the hijacking of an airplane, train, ship, bus, or other public conveyance.
15. The murder was committed for the purpose of concealing or attempting to conceal any felony offense.
16. The murder was committed for the purpose of causing or attempting to cause a person to refrain from initiating or aiding in the prosecution of a felony offense.
17. The murder was committed during the commission of a crime which is part of a pattern of criminal street gang activity.
18. The deliberate killing of any person in the commission of an act of terrorism. (Virginia, Tennessee, New Jersey, and Oklahoma)

The specific aggravating factors could vary from state to state. For example, Ohio lists as one aggravating factor "The offender, in the commission of the offense, purposefully caused the death of another who was under thirteen years of age at the time of the commission of the offense" (Ohio Revised Code [ORC] § 2929.04). In addition to states legislating certain aggravating factors, the federal government has its own list of aggravating factors that, if present, could result in imposition of the death penalty. The following list is taken from Title 18 and Title 21 of the United States Code Service (U.S.C.S.) and other sources.

Federal Aggravating Factors (from DPIC, also see 28 U.S.C.S. 848 and 18 U.S.C.S. 3592)

1. Murder related to the smuggling of aliens. (18 U.S.C. 1342)
2. Destruction of aircraft, motor vehicles, or related facilities resulting in death. (18 U.S.C. 32-34)
3. Murder committed during a drug-related drive-by shooting. (18 U.S.C. 36)
4. Murder committed at an airport serving international civil aviation. (18 U.S.C. 37)
5. Retaliatory murder of a member of the immediate family of law enforcement officials. (18 U.S.C. 115(b)(3) [by cross-reference to 18 U.S.C. 1111])

6. Civil rights offenses resulting in death. (18 U.S.C. 241, 242, 245, 247)
7. Murder of a member of Congress, an important executive official, or a Supreme Court Justice. (18 U.S.C. 351)
8. Death resulting from offenses involving transportation of explosives, destruction of government property, or destruction of property related to foreign or interstate commerce. (18 U.S.C. 844(d), (f), (i))
9. Murder committed by the use of a firearm during a crime of violence or a drug trafficking crime. (18 U.S.C 930)
10. Murder committed in a federal government facility. (18 U.S.C. 924(i))
11. Genocide. (18 U.S.C. 1091)
12. First degree murder. (18 U.S.C. 1111)
13. Murder of a federal judge or law enforcement official. (18 U.S.C. 1114)
14. Murder of a foreign official. (18 U.S.C. 1116)
15. Murder by a federal prisoner. (18 U.S.C. 1118)
16. Murder of a U.S. national in a foreign country. (18 U.S.C. 1119)
17. Murder by an escaped federal prisoner already sentenced to life imprisonment. (18 U.S.C. 1120)
18. Murder of a state or local law enforcement official or other person aiding in a federal investigation; murder of a state correctional officer. (18 U.S.C. 1121)
19. Murder during a kidnapping. (18 U.S.C. 1201)
20. Murder during a hostage taking. (18 U.S.C. 1203)
21. Murder of a court officer or juror. (18 U.S.C. 1503)
22. Murder with the intent of preventing testimony by a witness, victim, or informant. (18 U.S.C. 1512)
23. Retaliatory murder of a witness, victim, or informant. (18 U.S.C. 1513)
24. Mailing of injurious articles with intent to kill or injury resulting in death. (18 U.S.C. 1716)
25. Assassination or kidnapping resulting in the death of the President or Vice-President. (18 U.S.C. 1751 [by cross-reference to 18 U.S.C. 1111])
26. Murder for hire. (18 U.S.C. 1958)
27. Murder involved in a racketeering offense. (18 U.S.C. 1959)
28. Willful wrecking of a train resulting in death. (18 U.S.C. 1992)
29. Bank robbery-related murder or kidnapping. (18 U.S.C. 2113)
30. Murder related to a carjacking. (18 U.S.C. 2119)
31. Murder related to rape or child molestation. (18 U.S.C. 2245)
32. Murder related to sexual exploitation of children. (18 U.S.C. 2251)

33. Murder committed during an offense against maritime navigation. (18 U.S.C. 2280)
34. Murder committed during an offense against a maritime fixed platform. (18 U.S.C. 2281)
35. Terrorist murder of a U.S. national in another country. (18 U.S.C. 2332)
36. Murder by the use of a weapon of mass destruction. (18 U.S.C. 2332(a))
37. Murder involving torture. (18 U.S.C. 2340)
38. Murder related to a continuing criminal enterprise or related murder of a federal, state, or local law enforcement officer. (21 U.S.C. 848(e))
39. Death resulting from aircraft hijacking. (49 U.S.C. 1472-1473)
40. Espionage. (18 U.S.C. 794)
41. Treason. (18 U.S.C. 2381)
42. Trafficking in large quantities of illegal drugs. (18 U.S.C. 3591(b))
43. Attempting, authorizing, or advising the killing of any officer, juror, or witness in cases involving a continuing criminal enterprise, regardless of whether such killing actually occurs. (18 U.S.C. 3591(b)(2))

MITIGATING FACTORS

Following the decision in *Lockett*, most, though not all, state legislatures developed a list of statutory mitigating factors for the jury (or judge) to consider. Though the factors may differ from state to state, the defense, in every jurisdiction across the country, would be allowed to present any issue that might be seen as relevant to the jury's consideration of an appropriate sentence. The following is a list of typical legislative statutory mitigating factors.

Statutory Mitigating Factors

1. The defendant has no significant history of prior criminal activity.
2. The crime was committed while the defendant was under the influence of extreme mental or emotional disturbances.
3. The victim was a participant in or consented to the defendant's conduct.
4. The defendant was an accomplice in the crime committed by another person, and the defendant's participation was relatively minor.
5. The defendant acted under extreme distress or under the substantial domination of another person.

6. The capacity of the defendant to appreciate the criminality of his or her conduct or to conform his or her conduct to the requirements of law was substantially impaired.
7. The age of the defendant at the time of the crime.
8. At the time of the crime, the defendant was suffering from post-traumatic stress syndrome caused by violence or abuse by the victim.
9. A term of imprisonment is sufficient to defend and protect the people's safety from the defendant.
10. Any other factors that are relevant to the issue of whether the offender should be sentenced to death.

As a practical matter, most often the mitigation testimony hinges on this last factor which under *Wiggins* permits the defense to introduce any relevant testimony for the jury to consider.

As was the case with aggravating factors, the federal government has its own list of mitigating factors.

Federal Mitigating Factors
(18 U.S.C.S. 3592 and 21 U.S.C.S. 848)

In determining whether a sentence of death is to be imposed on a defendant, the finder of fact shall consider any mitigating factor, including the following:

1. *Impaired Capacity* — The defendant's capacity to appreciate the wrongfulness of the defendant's conduct or to conform conduct to the requirements of law was significantly impaired regardless of whether the capacity was so impaired as to constitute a defense to the charge.
2. *Duress* — The defendant was under unusual and substantial duress regardless of whether the duress was of such a degree as to constitute a defense to the charge.
3. *Minor Participation* — The defendant is punishable as a principal in the offense, which was committed by another, but the defendant's participation was relatively minor, regardless of whether the participation was so minor as to constitute a defense to the charge.
4. *Equally Culpable Defendants* — Another defendant or defendants, equally culpable in the crime, will not be punished by death.
5. *No Prior Criminal Record* — The defendant did not have a significant prior history of other criminal conduct.

6. *Disturbance* — The defendant committed the offense under severe mental or emotional disturbance.
7. *Victim's Consent* — The victim consented to the criminal conduct that resulted in the victim's death.
8. *Other Factors* — Other factors in the defendant's background, record, or character or any other circumstance of the offense that mitigate against imposition of the death sentence.

FUTURE DANGEROUSNESS AND AGGRAVATION AND MITIGATION

Texas and Oregon (an identical special issue) have adopted similar standards that ask the jury first to consider the issue of future dangerousness and culpability, then to consider mitigation. Texas, for example, requires jurors first to consider (a) whether there is a probability that the defendant would commit criminal acts of violence that would constitute a continuing threat to society and (b) whether the defendant actually caused the death of the deceased or did not actually cause the death of the deceased but intended to kill the deceased or another or anticipated that a human life would be taken. If the jury answers affirmatively (and it must be a unanimous vote on each), only then can it consider whether (taking into consideration all of the evidence, including the circumstances of the offense, the defendant's character and background, and the personal moral culpability of the defendant) there exists sufficient mitigation to warrant that a sentence of life imprisonment rather than a death sentence be imposed (see Texas Criminal Code 19.03 and Art. 3 7.071). Oregon has adopted nearly the same wording for its first-tier threshold test: (a) whether the conduct of the defendant that caused the death of the deceased was committed deliberately and with the reasonable expectation that death of the deceased or another would result; and (b) whether there is a probability that the defendant would commit criminal acts of violence that would constitute a continuing threat to society (ORS § 163.150, 2001). Only after an affirmative (and unanimous) finding on both of these issues can the jury move on to its second-tier analysis, which, of course, centers around the question of whether the defendant should be put to death.

Cunningham (in press) discusses the difficulties in the operational definitions of such terms as "future dangerousnes," "future acts of violence," "probability," and what constitutes a "continuing threat to society." These issues will be discussed in more detail in Chapter 11 on the Antisocial Personality Disorder.

JURY INSTRUCTIONS IN
DEATH PENALTY CASES

Jurors in death penalty cases have an obligation not only to determine guilt or innocence, but also to determine an appropriate punishment. The punishment in most states, as well as at the federal level, is the death penalty or a "life sentence" which can be handed down as life with no possibility of parole (LWOP), or as life with the stipulation that the defendants must serve a specified number of years (e.g., 20, 30, 40) before they can be considered for parole. The jury's sentencing recommendations are only for the specific aggravating circumstances. The court has the option of imposing additional time for any other convictions (e.g., rape, kidnapping, robbery, etc.). Before sentencing the defendant, jurors are given instructions by the court on how to interpret the aggravating and mitigating factors, how to apply the law, and how to "weigh" the evidence. Jury instructions, however, have never been easy to comprehend, and there have been a number of articles on this topic (see, for example, Butler & Moran, 2002; Diamond, 1993; Frank & Applegate, 1998; Luginbuhl & Middenhorf, 1988; and Lynch & Haney, 2000).

Courts provide instructions to jurors based on the recommendations of the defense attorneys and the prosecutors, but also taking into consideration previous case law. Judges have a certain amount of discretion in giving jury instructions, but they must be careful not to violate any previous rulings on the matter. Ohio provides an example, though not necessarily typical, of the way capital jury instructions might read. Assuming that the defendant has been convicted of aggravated murder with death penalty specifications, the jury, at the appropriate time, is then instructed as to the nature of mitigation and the procedure to follow in determining its presence or absence. Using Ohio Jury Instructions as a guide, jurors are given instructions similar to the following:

> Members of the jury, during the trial phase of this case, you heard evidence, testimony, and arguments of counsel and found the defendant guilty of aggravated murder with specifications. In this sentencing phase, those specifications will be addressed and called aggravating circumstances. You also heard during the trial phase some evidence, testimony, and arguments of counsel as to possible factors in mitigation of the death sentence. In this sentencing phase, which concerns only the determination of sentence, you will hear additional evidence, testimony, arguments of counsel, and perhaps a statement of the defendant. It is not necessary that the defendant

take the witness stand or make a statement. The defendant has a constitutional right not to testify or make a statement. The fact that the defendant does not testify or make a statement must not be considered for any purpose. The state will address the aggravating circumstances of which the defendant was found guilty, and the defense will address mitigating factors.

The aggravated murder itself is not an aggravating circumstance. Because you found that aggravating circumstances are present, the law provides the following sentencing options for your consideration: life imprisonment without parole eligibility for 30 full years, life imprisonment without parole eligibility for 25 years, life imprisonment without the possibility of parole, or death.

You are here today to consider which of these sentences to impose. The aggravating circumstances will be weighed against the mitigating factors that have or will be presented. Mitigating factors are factors about an individual or an offense that weigh in favor of a decision that a life sentence rather than a death sentence is appropriate. Mitigating factors are any factors that are relevant to the issue of whether the offender should be sentenced to death. Mitigating factors include, but are not limited to, the nature and circumstances of the offense; the history, character, and background of the defendant; and (in addition to the listed mitigating factors) any other factors that weigh in favor of a sentence other than death. This means that you are not limited to the specific mitigating factors that have been described to you. You should consider any other mitigating factors that weigh in favor of a sentence other than death.

Again, you will be deciding whether the state has proved beyond a reasonable doubt that the aggravating circumstances outweigh the mitigating factors. If you find the aggravating circumstances outweigh the mitigating factors, then you must find that the death sentence be imposed upon the defendant. However, if you find that the state did not prove beyond a reasonable doubt that the aggravating circumstances outweigh the mitigating factors, then you will enter a verdict imposing one of the life sentences, either life imprisonment without parole eligibility for 30 full years, or life imprisonment without the possibility of parole, whichever you deem appropriate. (Adapted and modified from Ohio Jury Instructions 503.011)

However, jurors are also instructed that the existence of any of the mitigating factors listed in this section does not preclude the imposition of a sentence of death but shall be weighed against the aggravating circumstances that the state proved, beyond a reasonable doubt, were present. Therefore even though mitigating factors exist, jurors may still decide in favor of death.

CASE EXAMPLE:
UNITED STATES v. McVEIGH

Of particular interest to highlight the jury's role in mitigation is the case of *United States v. McVeigh*. As most readers know, at 9:02 on the morning of April 19, 1995, a massive explosion tore apart the Alfred P. Murrah Federal Building in Oklahoma City, Oklahoma, killing a total of 168 people and injuring hundreds more. Timothy McVeigh was charged with numerous counts of aggravated murder, with the intent to kill two or more people specified as one of the aggravating circumstances. At sentencing, jurors were given insight into McVeigh's motivation for bombing the Murrah Building. The jury was presented, along with other information about McVeigh's background, the following factors that the defense hoped would be seen as mitigating:

1. Timothy McVeigh believed that the Bureau of Alcohol, Tobacco, Firearms and Explosives and the Federal Bureau of Investigation (FBI) were responsible for the deaths of everyone who lost their lives at Mt. Carmel, near Waco, Texas, between February 28 and April 19, 1993.
2. McVeigh chose the Murrah Building as the target because he believed that the orders for the attack at Waco emanated from that building and that the building housed various people who were directly involved in the Waco raid.
3. McVeigh believed that the increasing use of military-style force and tactics by federal law enforcement agencies against American citizens signaled movement toward a police state.
4. McVeigh believed that federal law enforcement agencies failed to take responsibility for their actions at Ruby Ridge and Waco and failed to punish those persons responsible. These beliefs dovetailed with his growing concerns regarding the existence of a police state and a loss of constitutional liberties.

Records show that the jury unanimously found present 7 of the 13 mitigating factors that McVeigh's defense team presented. These factors included the sincerity of McVeigh's beliefs regarding the government's actions at Waco, Texas, and Ruby Ridge, Idaho (where extremist groups believed that the FBI raid there in 1992 was a symbol of the federal government's brutality); the fact that McVeigh received the Bronze Star for his Army service; the point that "he is a patient and effective teacher when he is working in a supervisory role"; and the fact that he had no prior criminal record. Only two of the presented mitigating factors were rejected by each and every juror. In spite of these seemingly defense-oriented findings, the jury came to the conclusion that the aggravating circumstances of the offense outweighed the mitigating factors and decided that McVeigh should be put to death. After a period of appellate review, McVeigh waived any further review and was executed on June 11, 2001.

The jury's role at mitigation is to weigh the mitigation evidence presented by the defense and compare it to the aggravating circumstances of the offense. In most cases, mitigation focuses on the circumstances of the defendant's life, his or her psychosocial development, issues of abuse or neglect, or other understandable factors that caused the defendant to be damaged. None of these issues was of much significance in McVeigh's life. Most death penalty cases are not mass murders, as was the case here. It would have been highly unusual for jurors to recommend a life sentence. It is, perhaps, a good example of a jury finding mitigation, but not so compelling that it outweighed the aggravation (mass murder) specification.

Chapter 6

MITIGATION

HISTORY AND BACKGROUND OF MITIGATION

Furman paved the way for a number of cases that helped establish the principle of mitigation. When the Supreme Court struck down mandatory sentencing schemes (see *Woodson v. North Carolina*), it proceeded to make individualized sentencing a constitutional requirement when the punishment is death. Following *Lockett* (see below) the Court has consistently maintained that defense counsel can submit any evidence relevant to mitigation (see *Eddings v. Oklahoma; Penry v. Lynaugh; Skipper v. South Carolina*). The Court has stated that the failure to introduce mitigating evidence constitutes ineffective assistance of counsel and is grounds for reversal (see *Wiggins v. Smith; Williams v. Taylor*).

The *Lockett* Decision

Mitigation in death penalty cases essentially begins with the *Lockett* decision (*Lockett v. Ohio*) and is further clarified in *Eddings v. Oklahoma*. At the time of Lockett's sentencing, the Ohio death penalty statute required the trial judge to impose a death sentence unless, after "considering the nature and circumstances of the offense" and the defendant's "history, character, and condition," he found by a preponderance of the evidence that (a) the victim had induced or facilitated the offense, (b) it was unlikely that the defendant would have committed the offense but for the fact that she "was under duress, coercion, or strong provocation," or (c) the offense was "primarily the product of the defendant's psychosis or mental deficiency" (ORC §§

2929.03-2929.04 (B) (1975)). In sentencing Lockett to death, the trial judge concluded that the offense had not been primarily the product of psychosis or mental deficiency. Without specifically addressing the other two statutory mitigating factors, the judge said that he had "no alternative, whether [he liked] the law or not" but to impose the death penalty.

Lockett provides an example of a death penalty case where the death sentence was reversed by the Supreme Court but not the original conviction. Lockett claimed that she intended to kill no one. She maintained that she knew nothing about the plan to kill anyone (personal communication) and was across the street from the crime scene eating a hamburger. Excerpts from the case are presented below:

> Sandra Lockett was charged with aggravated murder and aggravated robbery making her eligible for the death penalty in Ohio. The State's case against her depended largely upon the testimony of a co-defendant, Al Parker. Apparently Lockett along with several other co-defendants had decided to rob a pawnshop in order to get money for a trip back to New Jersey. While Lockett sat in her car, the co-defendants entered the pawnshop and showed the owner some bullets. They asked to see a gun that would be a match for the bullets. The owner showed them a gun. They loaded it and then shot and killed the pawnshop owner. Fingerprints matched those of Al Parker.
>
> Parker was subsequently apprehended and charged with aggravated murder with specifications, an offense punishable by death, and aggravated robbery. He pled guilty to the murder charge and agreed to testify against Lockett and the other co-defendants. Lockett rejected a plea to voluntary manslaughter and a subsequent plea to aggravated murder without the death specification.
>
> At trial, Lockett's defense team stated that she had no knowledge of any plan to commit robbery and that she had been eating a hamburger across the street when the murder occurred. But based primarily on the testimony of Al Parker, the jury convicted Lockett of aggravated murder and robbery finding that she purposely had killed the pawnbroker while committing or attempting to commit aggravated robbery. The jury was further charged that one who "purposely aids, helps, associates himself or herself with another for the purpose of committing a crime is regarded as if he or she were the principal offender and is just as guilty as if the person performed every act constituting the offense. . . ."
>
> In accord with the Ohio statute, the trial judge requested a presentence report as well as psychiatric and psychological reports. The reports contained detailed information about Lockett's intelligence, character, and background. The psychiatric and psychological reports described her as a 21-year-old with low-average or average intelligence, and not suffering from a mental deficiency. One of the psy-

chologists reported that "her prognosis for rehabilitation" if returned to society was favorable. The presentence report showed that Lockett had committed no major offenses although she had a record of several minor ones as a juvenile and two minor offenses as an adult. It also showed that she had once used heroin but was receiving treatment at a drug abuse clinic and seemed to be "on the road to success" as far as her drug problem was concerned. It concluded that Lockett suffered no psychosis and was not mentally deficient.

After considering the reports and hearing argument on the penalty issue, the trial judge concluded that the offense had not been primarily the product of psychosis or mental deficiency and sentenced her to death. The judge declined to consider as a mitigating factor any other aspects of Lockett's background, character, or social history.

The Supreme Court concluded that the Eighth and Fourteenth Amendments require that the sentencer, in all but the rarest kind of capital case, not be precluded from considering, *as a mitigating factor*, any aspect of a defendant's character or record and any of the circumstances of the offense that the defendant proffers as a basis for a sentence less than death. Individualized sentencing had already been the established practice in noncapital cases. Given that the defendant may be sentenced to death (a penalty clearly different from all other penalties), the Court concluded that an individualized decision is essential in capital cases. The Court stated that individualized sentencing was important "in order to treat each defendant with that degree of respect due the uniqueness of the individual."

Sandra Lockett spent 18 years in prison prior to her release. She has been a frequent guest speaker at local colleges and universities. In 2002, she returned to prison following a probation violation but was paroled again in July of 2003.

PRACTICAL ASPECTS
OF MITIGATION

Mitigation is a concept often foreign even to those who participate in the legal process. Some defense attorneys in capital cases have been quoted as saying, "I don't believe in mitigation." Those outside of the legal system typically do not understand what mitigation is or why it matters. Cunningham and Reidy (2001) point out that the central component of mitigation is an analysis of the defendant's moral culpability as opposed to criminal responsibility. Criminal responsibility would have already been determined at the factfinding phase of the trial and therefore has little relevance at mitigation, though the prosecutor would certainly disagree. The question at mitigation, therefore, focuses on the interaction of those biological, psychological, or social factors that might have shaped a defendant's life or affected his or her value system, and the capacity to make mature and reasonable choices. Cunningham (2003) refers to those factors that have diminished or shaped the moral development of the defendant, thus affecting the "choices" that he or she makes. Moral culpability suggests that there are a number of factors that might make someone more or less culpable. For example, children are not to be considered as equally culpable as adults. For a variety of reasons, punishments for children are not the same as those for adults. Likewise, mentally retarded adults are not held to the same moral culpability as higher functioning adults. The purpose of mitigation is to provide the jury with a full consideration of evidence that might temper the risk of an "unguided emotional response" to the aggravating circumstances. Mitigation is essential if the jury is to give a "reasoned moral response to the defendant's background, character, and crime" (*Penry v. Lynaugh*). The defense attorney's goal is to provide sufficient information, often through psychological testimony, about the client's unique life circumstances in order to consider a punishment other than death.

Mitigation normally begins with an extensive interview and evaluation of the defendant. Stetler, Burt, and Johnson (1998) stated that mitigation requires a multigenerational inquiry into the genetic predispositions and environmental influences that molded the defendant's personality and life. Mitigation then becomes a documented record of the specific impairments, deficits, and disorders not only of the defendant but also of any family members. The failure to do a thorough mitigation investigation has resulted in successful "ineffective assistance of counsel" claims in capital cases (*Williams v. Taylor*).

Research suggests that jurors tend to focus most on factors that diminish the defendant's individual responsibility for his or her actions, such as mental retardation, diminished capacity, extreme emotional or mental disturbance, or residual doubt. However, Garvey (1998) pointed out that jurors have little patience with a defendant's stated drug and alcohol history though they may give some limited weight to factors such as poverty or child abuse. Indeed, jurors often view drug and alcohol abuse as an aggravating factor rather than a mitigating factor. What a defense attorney might view as "mitigating" a juror might view in an entirely different way.

The strategy for attorneys representing capital defendants is, in most cases, to save the client's life. It should come as no surprise that the majority of capitally charged defendants are, in fact, guilty — though not necessarily guilty of the aggravating death specifications. The attorney's job at sentencing is to put together an effective mitigation team using the services of numerous mental health professionals, including psychologists, neuropsychologists, psychiatrists, social workers, drug and alcohol experts, and other specialists.

The responsibility of developing a mitigation strategy belongs to the defense attorneys. Yet the task of collecting records and developing a psychosocial developmental history of the defendant usually falls to a social worker (mitigation specialist), a forensic psychologist, and any other experts, depending on the case.

Schroeder (2003) summarized the social worker's role in death penalty mitigation and discusses the specific tasks of a mitigation specialist. She states that the mitigation specialist functions as the liaison between the attorney and the defendant, the defendant's family, and other potential defense witnesses. She describes a model for mitigation investigation based on the work of Norton (1992), Stetler (1999), and Wheelan (1996). Mitigation investigation includes the multidimensional approach and an assessment of the defendant and of his or her family in order to develop an "ecological" understanding in the larger context of his or her unique environmental and cultural circumstances and perspectives. This process normally begins shortly after the defendant's arrest and indictment. Such an investigation requires a significant amount of time in gathering any and all records and documents that form an objective basis in developing a complete psychological and social understanding of the defendant.

In summary, the preparation for the mitigation phase of a capital case is a long and tedious task. The preparation involves extensive research into the background of the defendant, with special attention to cultural differences. Mitigation investigation includes a synthesis of all available records from schools, mental health clinics, juvenile authorities, hospitals, psychologists, school psychologists, social workers, psychiatrists, employers, probation officers, and so on. The collection of records is vitally important in the area of intellectual and emotional development, sexual and marital development, medical history, and other collaborative material. Any preparation for the mitigation phase should include the following:

I.   Obtaining the following background information regarding the defendant:

A. developmental experiences
B. family dynamics and functioning
C. parenting capacities in the family of the defendant
D. academic capacities and achievements as well as failures

     E. work experiences including relationships with coworkers
       as well as job skills
     F. interpersonal relationships and social adjustments
     G. sexual and marital history
     H. medical history
     I. psychological functioning across the defendant's lifetime
     J. issues relating to cultural and social differences.

II.   This information can only be obtained by lengthy interviews
    with:

     A. family members
     B. neighbors
     C. employers
     D. teachers
     E. significant people in the defendant's life
     F. medical and psychiatric professionals
     G. cultural experts who might be able to provide valuable in-
       formation given a defendant's particular circumstances

AMERICAN BAR ASSOCIATION'S GUIDELINES FOR MITIGATION*

In 2003, the American Bar Association published its own guidelines for the appointment and performance of defense counsel in death
penalty cases. The guidelines state that counsel has an "obligation to
conduct thorough and independent investigations relating to the issues of both guilt and penalty." That investigation includes, but is not
limited to, the following:

> Counsel's duty to investigate and present mitigating evidence
> is now well established. The duty to investigate exists regardless of
> the expressed desires of a client. Nor may counsel "sit idly by, think-
> ing that investigation would be futile." Counsel cannot responsibly
> advise a client about the merits of different courses of action, the
> client cannot make informed decisions, and counsel cannot be sure
> of the client's competency to make such decisions, unless counsel
> has first conducted a thorough investigation with respect to both
> phases of the case.
>
> Because the sentencer in a capital case must consider in mitiga-
> tion, "anything in the life of the defendant which might militate
> against the appropriateness of the death penalty for the defendant,"

* From "ABA Guidelines for the Appointment and Performance of Defense Counsel in Death Penalty
Cases (rev. ed.)" by American Bar Association, 2003, *Hofstra Law Review, 31*, pp. 1021-1025. Copyright © 2003 by the American Bar Association. Reprinted by permission.

"penalty phase preparation requires extensive and generally unparalleled investigation into personal and family history." At least in the case of the client, this begins with the moment of conception [i.e., undertaking representation of the capital defendant]. Counsel needs to explore:

(1) Medical history (including hospitalizations, mental and physical illness or injury, alcohol and drug use, pre-natal and birth trauma, malnutrition, developmental delays, and neurological damage);

(2) Family and social history (including physical, sexual or emotional abuse; family history of mental illness, cognitive impairments, substance abuse, or domestic violence; poverty, familial instability, neighborhood environment and peer influence); other traumatic events such as exposure to criminal violence, the loss of a loved one, or a natural disaster; experiences of racism or other social or ethnic bias; cultural or religious influences; failures of government or social intervention (*e.g.*, failure to intervene or provide necessary services, placement in poor quality foster care or juvenile detention facilities);

(3) Educational history (including achievement, performance, behavior, and activities), special educational needs (including cognitive limitations and learning disabilities) and opportunity or lack thereof, and activities;

(4) Military service (including length and type of service, conduct, special training, combat exposure, health and mental health services);

(5) Employment and training history (including skills and performance, and barriers to employability);

(6) Prior juvenile and adult correctional experience (including conduct while under supervision, in institutions of education or training, and regarding clinical services);

The mitigation investigation should begin as quickly as possible, because it may affect the investigation of first phase defenses (*e.g.*, by suggesting additional areas for questioning police officers or other witnesses), decisions about the need for expert evaluations (including competency, mental retardation, or insanity), motion practice, and plea negotiations. . . .

It is necessary to locate and interview the client's family members (who may suffer from some of the same impairments as the client), and virtually everyone else who knew the client and his family, including neighbors, teachers, clergy, case workers, doctors, correctional, probation or parole officers, and others. Records — from courts, government agencies, the military, employers, etc. —

can contain a wealth of mitigating evidence, documenting or providing clues to childhood abuse, retardation, brain damage, and/or mental illness, and corroborating witnesses' recollections. Records should be requested concerning not only the client, but also his parents, grandparents, siblings, and children. A multi-generational investigation . . . frequently discloses significant patterns of family dysfunction and may help establish or strengthen a diagnosis or underscore the hereditary nature of a particular impairment. The collection of corroborating information from multiple sources — a time-consuming task — is important wherever possible to ensure the reliability and thus the persuasiveness of the evidence.

RESOURCES FOR CLIENT RECORDS

The following is a list of records normally gathered in a capital case. Records should be obtained for all family members, living or dead. Occasionally this process can be expedited with a court order or a subpoena.

I. AGENCIES

    A. Foster Homes

    B. Children's Services

    C. Drug and/or Alcohol Treatment Programs

    D. Mental Health Clinics or Centers

    E. Psychiatric Treatment Facilities for Children, Adolescents, and Adults

    F. Department of Youth Services (Group Homes, etc.)

II. MEDICAL

    A. Hospitals

        1. In-Patient

        2. Out-Patient

        3. Emergency Room

    B. Family Physicians

        1. Family Doctor

        2. Attending Physicians (e.g., Emergency Room)

        3. Medical Clinics (Urgent Care)

III. EDUCATIONAL

    A. Pre-School and/or Head Start Program

    B. Elementary, Middle Schools, and High Schools

        1. Public

        2. Private

        3. Special Programs (Learning Disabled Classes, etc.)

    C. Post-High School, Vocational, Training, and College

IV. JUVENILE AND/OR ADULT CRIMINAL RECORDS

    A. County Juvenile Records

        1. Formal Charges/Convictions
        2. Placements in Youth Services Programs, Group Homes, Detention, and So Forth
        3. Probation Records
        4. Records of Dismissed Charges
        5. Referrals to Other Agencies
        6. Psychological Evaluations

    B. Adult Criminal Records

        1. Formal Charges/Convictions
        2. Probation or Sentence to Prison (Name of Correctional Facility)
        3. Parole Records/Furlough
        4. Programs Completed in Prison

V. EMPLOYMENT

    A. Past Employers

        1. Part-Time or Full-Time
        2. Adolescent and Adult Jobs

    B. Job Training Programs

VI. MILITARY

    A. Branch of Service Enlisted (Army, Navy, Air Force, Marines, National Guard, Coast Guard)
    B. Date and Place of Enlistment
    C. Rank Achieved
    D. Places Stationed During Enlistment
    E. Commanding Officers' Names
    F. Names of Relatives Who Served in the Military

    Note: To get past military records, send authorization and release along with identifying information to:

    National Personnel Records Center
    (Navy, Army, Air Force, etc.) — whichever is appropriate
    9700 Page Avenue
    St. Louis, MO 63132-5100

VII. RELIGIOUS INSTITUTIONS

    A. Churches
    B. Names of Clergy and/or Volunteer Staff (Sunday School Teacher, etc.)
    C. Church Groups/Camps or Other Church-Related Organizations

VIII. MISCELLANEOUS

    A. Other Organizations

        1. Sports Teams/Coaches
        2. Political
        3. Alcoholics Anonymous/Narcotics Anonymous
        4. Charity

    B. Birth Certificates
    C. Prenatal Medical Records
    D. School Records
    E. Marriage Records
    F. Death Certificates
    G. Drug or Alcohol Treatment Records
    H. Criminal Records
     I. Juvenile Court Records
    J. Employment Records
    K. Workers' Compensation
    L. Social Security Records (for Disability)
    M. Military Records
    N. Jail and/or Prison Records
    O. Medical Records
    P. Psychiatric and Psychological Records Including Raw Data
    Q. Court Files for Any Litigation Involving Defendant

RISK FACTORS FOR
VIOLENCE AND DELINQUENCY

The United States Department of Justice has identified a number of risk factors for violence and delinquency in the community. These factors may serve as a guide for organizing mitigation and testifying at trial. (See U.S. Department of Justice, 1995.)

Risk Factors From Conception to Age 6

- Perinatal difficulties
- Minor physical abnormalities
- Brain damage
- Family history of criminal behavior and substance abuse
- Family management problems
- Family conflict
- Parental attitudes favorable toward, and parental involvement in, crime and substance abuse

Risk Factors From Age 6 Through Adolescence

- Extreme economic deprivation
- Community disorganization and low neighborhood attachment

- Transitions and mobility
- Availability of firearms
- Media portrayals of violence
- Family management problems
- Family conflict
- Parental attitudes favorable toward, and parental involvement in, crime and substance abuse
- Early and persistent antisocial behavior
- Academic failure
- Lack of commitment to school
- Alienation and rebelliousness
- Association with peers who engage in delinquency and violence
- Favorable attitudes towards delinquent and violent behaviors
- Constitutional factors (e.g., low intelligence, hyperactivity, attention-deficit disorders)

The Office of Juvenile Justice and Delinquency Prevention (OJJDP) coordinated an analysis of 66 studies, research reports, and longitudinal data on the individual, family, school/peer-related, and community/neighborhood risk factors for youth violence. The report concluded that there is a cumulative impact: the larger the number of risk factors the youth was exposed to, the greater the probability of violent behavior in the community. In addition, the following factors were identified as predictors of youth violence (see Hawkins et al., 2000):

Individual Risk Factors

- Hyperactivity, concentration problems, restlessness, and risk taking
- Aggressiveness
- Early initiation of violent behavior
- Involvement in other forms of antisocial behavior
- Beliefs and attitudes favorable to deviant or antisocial behavior

Family Risk Factors

- Parental criminality
- Child maltreatment
- Poor family management practices
- Low levels of parental involvement
- Poor family bonding and family contact
- Residential mobility
- Parental attitudes favorable to substance abuse and violence
- Parent-child separation

School Risk Factors

- Academic failure
- Low bonding to school
- Truancy and dropping out of school
- Frequent school transitions
- High delinquency school rates

Peer-Related Risk Factors

- Delinquent siblings
- Delinquent peers
- Gang membership

Community and Neighborhood Risk Factors

- Poverty
- Community disorganization (crime, drug-selling, gangs, poor housing)
- Availability of drugs and firearms
- Neighborhood adults involved in crime
- Exposure to violence and racial prejudice

JUVENILE AND ADOLESCENT OFFENDERS

The factors mentioned previously and others may contribute to the delay in maturity seen in any capital defendant, but particularly in youthful or juvenile defendants — a group that makes up a significant proportion of defendants. According to the DOJ, by the end of 2002, 13% of those sentenced to death were under 20 years of age, 40.1% were under 25, and 62.7% were under 30. The unique circumstances of the juvenile and adolescent capital defendant present additional mitigation tasks for the forensic psychologist and would normally require a neuropsychological evaluation. Steinberg and Scott (2003) describe the developmental immaturity and deficiencies in decision-making abilities rendering juveniles particularly vulnerable to the influence of coercive circumstances. Combined with the corruptive influences of family or community, juveniles are thus "more susceptible to influence, less future oriented, less risk aversive, and less able to manage their impulses and behavior, and that these differences have a neurobiological basis" (p. 1013).

Appendix A (pp. 141-142) is a list of key areas to explore with the defendant, his or her family, and any other possible sources of information. Prior to preparing a report or to testifying, one should take into consideration any relevant information from those sources listed.

Chapter 7

GETTING STARTED ON A CAPITAL CASE

BASICS

The decision to accept an appointment to a capital case is a serious one. Evaluators must decide if they want the responsibility for such a case. Though the psychologist or psychiatrist may be asked only to do a competency-to-stand-trial evaluation, jurors may still consider the results from that evaluation as a basis for their recommendation of life or death (see *Estelle v. Smith*). Very limited participation may be viewed by appellate courts as sufficient to deny relief on psychological issues. Evaluations of any issue in a capital case can have far reaching ramifications and call for particular care.

Capital cases are highly publicized. Though this should not preclude accepting a referral, these cases may expose the evaluator to unwanted publicity. Capital cases are profoundly different from all other types of forensic evaluations. The gravity of the determination is unparalleled, the intensity of the advocacy is much greater, and the ethical pitfalls of the assessment and evaluation are more complex. For one thing, as a result of appellate review and postconviction petitions, capital cases may remain active for more than 20 years, with the original psychological evaluation cited as a basis for an appeal. In addition, the evaluation may be the subject of intense scrutiny by other attorneys, their experts, and by the courts.

After agreeing to the appointment, psychologists should clarify with counsel their role including the evaluations to be considered (e.g., criminal responsibility, competency to stand trial, diminished capacity, etc.). Psychologists should also make it clear that they are participants, not members of the "team" — whether it be for the defense or the prosecution. (The concept of the defense team is discussed in Chapter 8 and Chapter 13.) The psychologist should meet with the mitigation specialist as soon as possible in order to delineate each other's roles and to share information. The attorneys, mitigation specialist, and psychologist should have an initial meeting with the defendant and let him or her know what is expected of everyone. It is important to develop at least a provisional conceptualization of the scope of the consultation in order to recommend other experts to the defense counsel. These might include mitigation specialists, anthropologists, criminologists, sociologists/social workers, neuropsychologists, neurologists, mental retardation experts, endocrinologists, drug and alcohol experts, cult experts, or battered women experts. One cannot be expected to know everything. Again, at the risk of being redundant, role clarification with defense counsel is extremely important.

RECORDS

All available records should be given to the psychologist, and every effort should be made to collect any other potentially important documents. Many defendants have prior convictions and have served time in prison. Records should be requested from probation officers, parole officers, and the various Departments of Correction. This does, however, present a problem in some situations. It may be the strategy of defense counsel and a right of the defendant not to inform the jury of the defendant's prior convictions. If the psychologist has prepared a written report that has relied on prison records or presentence evaluations, or intends to present testimony based on those records, there is then a risk to the defense strategy that the psychologist, in either direct or cross-examination, may reveal this information to the jury. The result may be a mistrial, a conviction, or a death sentence.

Revealing a defendant's prior criminal record may also undermine a defense tactic of residual doubt. Consider a defendant charged with rape and murder who has a prior conviction for rape. A jury that learns of that prior rape is more likely to have a lower threshold for conviction and a less difficult task at sentencing. The psychologist, however, has the ethical and legal obligation to testify truthfully. It may be useful to have the judge rule on the admissibility of such testimony prior to the psychologist's taking the witness stand. Yet it is also the right of the defendant, in many jurisdictions, not to have prior offenses introduced to the jury. Psychologists must be careful in that they have an obligation to practice in ways that do not diminish the defendant's constitutional rights. The dilemma of the completeness of the information provided to the psychologist is normally resolved by the focus of the evaluation. The evaluation is not necessarily a comprehensive psychological evaluation. It is an evaluation of mitigating factors and potentially violence-risk assessment. Neither of these requires exploration of aggravation, prior unadjudicated acts, or other examples of how the developmental damage was played out in criminal conduct (Cunningham, personal communication, 2003). Informed consent requires the psychologist to discuss with the attorney (and the defendant), in advance, the implications of what information the psychologist needs in addressing specific psycholegal issues in order that everyone can make an informed decision about whether and how to proceed.

In other instances, attorneys may conceal prison records (and sometimes other evaluations perceived to be negative) from their mental health experts in an effort to avoid disclosing that information to a jury through testimony. This also presents a dilemma because the psychologist is then put into a position of offering testimony without all available information, thus comprising the duty to be thorough in the psychological evaluation. This again relates to the original question of role clarification. Though it is the psychologist's responsibility to review all the records in keeping with the standards of the profession and the Specialty Guidelines for Forensic Psychologists (1991), the attorneys clearly set the parameters for a trial or mitigation strategy in case they choose to call the psychologist as a witness or not.

SETTING FOR THE FORENSIC EVALUATION

Most evaluations of capital defendants occur in a jail or prison. One should insist that the jail or prison provide a professional setting for the interview and evaluation in order to conform as much as possible to a standardized assessment. This can usually be arranged through the jail or prison warden, or on occasion, with the help of the judge issuing a court order requiring such accommodations. Otherwise, one's testimony can be attacked based on the lack of standardized assessment.

JUST THE FACTS

It is sometimes a difficult decision to pressure the defendant for details about the alleged criminal act, especially early in the interviewing process. Counsel must lend some guidance on this issue. Though the actual circumstances of the alleged offense are obviously important, counsel may have reasons to limit such discussions. For example, if the trial strategy is an "alibi" defense, then the facts of the case are less important because the defendant will be maintaining his or her innocence. In a criminal responsibility assessment, the facts of the case are extremely important in determining the *mens rea* portion of the evaluation. On other occasions, defendants will simply claim their innocence. Again, informed consent is key. Defense counsel sets the parameters. If the psychologist were not given information about the instant offense, then the testimony would be limited in opinions regarding mental disturbance at the time of the offense.

A WORD OF CAUTION

The evaluation of a capital defendant may take place over many months and sometimes years. It is not unusual to spend over 100 hours evaluating the defendant, working with defense attorneys, family members, and other experts. After doing hundreds of these types of evaluations, one comes to the conclusion that psychologists usually see the defendant at his or her best and that the victim saw the defendant at his or her worst. One must maintain professional objectivity and integrity — whether retained by the defense or the prosecution. This is often difficult when one considers the heinousness of the offense, "team mentality" pressures, overidentification with the defendant, a strong interest in the case outcome, or public pressures. It is a daunting task.

COVER LETTER TO ATTORNEYS

It is good practice in forensic evaluations, and especially important in capital cases, to provide a cover letter to attorneys. The letter should include a statement of one's background, training, education, publications, and experience. The letter should address the amount of time necessary to review historical data or records and to perform an independent psychological evaluation of the defendant. Normally, this process takes many months and is not something that can be done at the last minute. If the court is pressing for a speedy trial, the psychologist should submit an affidavit outlining the reasons that it is unreasonable to expect a thorough evaluation within the stated time constraints. This affidavit would then become part of the record for potential later review. Role clarification is also important. The letter should state what the expected role is (mitigation testimony, criminal responsibility, competency to stand trial, or some other function) with a clear understanding that these roles should normally not all be handled by the same professional. Finally, the amount of time and fee structure should be stated. Hourly rates are usually based on (a) the interview and direct evaluation of the defendant; (b) consultation with attorneys; (c) interviews with family, teachers, or other relevant third parties; (d) review of records; (e) literature review; (f) consultation with other experts; (g) preparation of any report, affidavit, or court exhibit; and (h) testimony. The number of hours in a typical case usually exceeds 50. Arrangements for travel expenses should be clarified. At all times, one should be aware of both Specialty Guidelines for Forensic Psychologists (1991) and the American Psychological Association's Ethical Principles for Psychologists and Code of Conduct (APA, 2002).

Chapter 8

THE ROLE OF THE PSYCHOLOGIST IN DEATH PENALTY LITIGATION

Psychologists may serve in any number of roles in death penalty litigation. Since these cases may last more than 20 years from trial to execution or relief, there are many opportunities to participate as a defense- or state-retained expert. The following discussion assumes, however, that most of the referrals came from defense attorneys, though the prosecution may use experts in similar ways. To begin, a psychologist can serve either as consultant or as the testifying expert but not both (Cunningham & Reidy, 2001).

CONSULTANT

The role of consultant suggests that no testimony will be required. As a consultant the psychologist may perform any of the following tasks:

1. **Review of Records.** Perhaps the most important task in death penalty litigation is the review of all available records. These records, which often cover the life span of the defendant, normally precede the alleged criminal act and include any of those records listed in the chapter on mitigation (see Chapter 6). Records form the basis for developing a psychosocial history of the defendant in order to give the jury a thorough understanding of the defendant, his or her background, the crime, and any relevant aggravating or mitigating factors. In this role, the psychologist or other mental health expert can provide the attorney

with a psychosocial assessment and those factors that might assist mitigation or trial strategy.

2. **Jury Selection.** There has been considerable research on jury selection in general as well as in capital litigation. The vast majority of capital defendants are indigent and, therefore, unable to afford the expense of a jury selection expert. Yet, some courts are willing to provide attorneys with jury selection experts. Capital cases are unique in criminal law since jurors must be "death qualified" in order to serve (see *Wainwright v. Witt*). The "neutrality" of death qualified juries has been the subject of a number of articles beginning with the 1984 special edition of *Law and Human Behavior* (see also Diamond, 1993; Elliot & Robinson, 1991) and summarized in Allen, Mabry, and McKelton (1998). Bennett and Hirschhorn (1993) wrote on the systematic selection of jury selection in both civil and criminal litigation (see also Kovera, Dickinson, & Cutler in Goldstein, 2003). Actual jury selection in capital cases can last as long as several months or as short as a single day. Experts on jury selection may also work with focus groups, shadow juries, mock juries, or the actual *voir dire* of potential jurors.

3. **Assessment Without Testimony.** Attorneys may want an evaluation of their client without disclosing those results to the prosecution. The results of that assessment may help develop a defense strategy either for trial or for mitigation. The prosecution, on the other hand, will rarely have an opportunity for such a consulting expert evaluation unless given permission by defense counsel. That is not likely to happen unless there is an issue of competency or sanity. The state would not get a consulting expert at that juncture either, only an expert to address the specific issues. Yet the prosecution may also use psychologists to review any available records as stated previously and assist the prosecution in formulating their own trial or response to mitigation strategy.

TEACHING OR RESEARCH-BASED TESTIMONY
(i.e., Eyewitness Identification, Coerced or False Confession)

Some of the most significant work in psychology has been research on the reliability of eyewitness identification and on coerced or false confessions. This type of testimony is particularly important when other physical evidence is lacking and the only evidence for the prosecution is based on an eyewitness or from a defendant's confession. There have been numerous accounts of defendants who were wrongly sentenced to death row (see, for example, Protess and Warden's, *A Promise of Justice*, 1998). The work by Wells and Loftus and others has spawned a significant amount of research and controversy in both the areas of eyewitness identification and repressed memories (see Loftus, 1996; Loftus & Ketcham, 1994; Wells, 1995).

MULTIPLE ROLES

Though a psychologist may have expertise in a number of different areas (e.g., forensic psychology, death penalty mitigation, jury selection, and eyewitness identification), he or she must, whenever possible, limit involvement to only one forensic evaluation function. On the other hand, most courts provide very little money for experts, and attorneys will attempt to use the expert as best they can to assist their defense. One should not be the consultant and a testifying expert for the same case.

"THE TEAM APPROACH"

Death penalty cases typically involve a group of professionals: attorneys, criminal investigators, mitigation specialists, and psychologists. Defense attorneys often refer to the "defense team" and assume that the psychologist is one of the players. Goldstein (2001) has cautioned psychologists against this concept and the inherent hazard in adopting the "team" approach in a capital case. Once identified as a member of the defense team, a jury is likely to see the psychologist as biased. In addition, the expert may come to see himself or herself as part of the team, thus overidentifying with the team, losing objectivity and/or professionalism. Such identification could result in inaccurate testimony. Psychologists must be aware of these pressures and should state to the defense or prosecuting attorneys that they will provide an objective, unbiased evaluation. The decision to use the results of that evaluation is then left to the attorneys.

THE MITIGATION SPECIALIST

A critically important professional in capital litigation is the mitigation specialist. The mitigation specialist typically comes from a background in social work but may also be a psychologist, criminal investigator, or even an attorney with training in social work. The mitigation specialist is responsible for researching and collecting records, extensive social histories and interviews with the defendant and the family, relevant witnesses, and assisting counsel in a variety of ways. Ordinarily, the mitigation specialists do not testify at sentencing. Therefore, they can effectively serve as a firewall between the attorneys and the experts providing the defense with a mechanism to gather a wealth of information without risk of introducing these materials at trial. The attorney can then make a strategic decision to introduce the gathered material or not.

SPECIFIC EVALUATIONS

Competency

A fairly common role for psychologists in the capital litigation is the evaluation of the defendant for competency to stand trial. Competency evaluations normally are performed prior to trial but may be requested at any time, if warranted. Other types of competency evaluations include the defendant's competency to waive jury, competency to waive the right to counsel, competency to enter a plea, competency to waive appeals, and competency to be executed. Since the ruling in *Godinez v. Moran*, the assumption is that if the defendant is competent to stand trial then the defendant is competent in most other areas. Yet the reverse of this also must be considered. If the defendant is not competent to waive appeals, not competent to enter a plea, or not competent to waive counsel, then one might assume that the defendant is, therefore, not competent to stand trial even though the defendant has "sufficient present ability to consult with his attorney with a reasonable degree of rational understanding and a rational as well as factual understanding of the proceedings against him" (*Dusky v. United States*). It follows that all aspects of "competency" should be explored because once the court rules on competency, that decision is likely to hold for the remainder of the trial.

Criminal Responsibility

Though criminal responsibility (sanity) evaluations are routine in the practice of forensic psychology, the vast majority of these defendants are found to be sane. This is also the case for capital defendants. The research indicates that when the defense of insanity is raised, "death qualified" juries are more skeptical of the insanity plea and more likely to convict than non-death qualified juries (see Ellsworth et al., 1984).

However, though the insanity plea may be rejected at trial, evidence of the mental state of the defendant may be raised again at mitigation. Psychologists may be requested to testify both at trial and, if the defendant is found guilty, at mitigation. At mitigation, most states permit testimony concerning the defendant's state of mind at the time of the criminal offense for which he or she has been found guilty and whether he or she was either able to appreciate the wrongfulness of the conduct or conform that conduct to the requirements of the law. The language is usually similar to the wording for insanity, but because the defendant has already been convicted, he or she is now technically the "offender." The issue of the defendant's mental state at the time of the criminal act is a factor only to be weighed against the aggravating factors and does not lessen the defendant's culpability. Attorneys must make a tactical decision with regard to the use of the insanity plea. They must decide whether its use comprises a mitigation strategy that might be perceived by the jury as redundant. It is possible that if the jury rejects the insanity plea, then they might also reject the mental illness claim at mitigation.

Other Evaluations

Depending on the jurisdiction, psychologists may be called upon to testify with respect to such issues as diminished capacity, the effects of alcoholic dependency or the effects of alcoholic parents on early child development, the effects of early childhood trauma on brain or neurotransmitter development, risk assessment or future dangerousness, attention-deficit/hyperactivity disorder and its relationship to the antisocial personality disorder, posttraumaumatic stress disorder, or any of the personality disorders. In essence, a psychologist may be asked to testify about any issue relevant to whether the jury should recommend death as opposed to life. Finally, any of these issues may be the subject of testimony at any stage of the proceedings, including pretrial motions, the trial, the mitigation hearing, appellate review, postconviction, or federal habeas.

THE CASE OF THE
CONVERSE ALL-STARS

The following is an example of a postconviction petition and affidavit. This affidavit was filed 4 years after the conviction. The defendant, William Wayne Green (names have been changed) was charged with the aggravated murder and robbery of his landlord. On January 29, 1985, the body of James Smith was discovered on his kitchen floor. It was determined that he had been stabbed 22 times, puncturing his left lung and right ventricle. Police discovered two shoeprints at the crime scene. These shoeprints had been found around the victim and were composed of the victim's blood. Both of the shoeprints were of a left tennis shoe bearing the distinctive pattern found only on Converse All-Star tennis shoes. The police arrested Green, who was wearing Converse All-Stars. Even though it had been snowing, Green told the police that those were the only shoes he owned.

Green was convicted of aggravated murder and robbery, and the jury returned a verdict of death that the judge imposed. On appeal, the court affirmed Green's conviction because circumstantial evidence revealed he was the only person who could have committed the crime and that the trial court did not commit reversible error in its rulings. The death sentence was affirmed by the Ohio Supreme Court, stating that the aggravating factors outweighed the mitigating factors beyond a reasonable doubt.

EXAMPLE OF A
POSTCONVICTION AFFIDAVIT

IN THE COURT OF COMMON PLEAS

DARBY COUNTY, OHIO

STATE OF OHIO,

    Plaintiff-Respondent,

    Case No. XXX

-vs-

WILLIAM WAYNE GREEN

    Defendant-Petitioner. :

AFFIDAVIT OF JAMES R. EISENBERG, PH.D.

IN THE STATE OF OHIO

COUNTY OF LAKE, SS:

I, James R. Eisenberg, being first duly sworn according to law, states the following:

1) I am a psychologist, licensed to practice in Ohio since 1978.

2) I am a Diplomate of the American Board of Forensic Psychology and a Diplomate of the American Board of Professional Psychology. I am Professor of Psychology at Lake Erie College.

3) For the past 10 years, I have been the Court Psychologist for the Lake County Forensic Psychiatric Clinic, and I continue to serve in that capacity for the Lake County Court of Common Pleas.

4) In the course of my employment with the Psychiatric Clinic and my practice as a Forensic Psychologist, I have evaluated more than 2,000 criminal defendants including approximately 60 capitally charged defendants.

5) I have testified for the prosecution, defense and for the court. I am quite familiar with the type of preparation required for capital cases, especially mitigation of the death penalty.

6) The preparation for the mitigation phase of a capital case is a long and tedious task. The preparation involves extensive research into the background of the defendant and includes a collection of all available records from schools, mental health clinics, juvenile authorities, hospitals, psychologists, school psychologists, psychiatrists, social workers, employers, probation officers, and so on. The collection of records is vitally important in the area of intellectual and emotional development, sexual and marital development, medical history, and other collaborative material. In my experience, these records often do exist, but it takes months to collect them. This is a task which often requires much foot work, phone calls, follow-up letters, travel, more phone calls, and more letters. Though the attorney is responsible for collection of these records, he or she may delegate that responsibility to someone else. The person most qualified for this particular task is a trained mitigation specialist whose interviewing skills and educational background are appropriate. This process must begin months before trial in order to have an effective and meaningful understanding of the defendant and the crime.

7) If mitigation begins following the factfinding phase, the defendant is typically angry and uncooperative. These attitudes and behaviors are usually interpreted as a basis for a diagnosis of antisocial personality. Evaluation of the defendant must therefore begin months before he or she goes to trial in

order to gain a full understanding of psychological, emotional, and social functioning.

8) In addition to the collection of records, additional information must also be pursued:

a. Extensive interviews of family members, including parents, stepparents, siblings, aunts, uncles, grandparents, cousins, as well as neighbors, professional associations (physicians, etc.), court personnel, and the like. In my experience, individuals charged with capital offenses have extremely dysfunctional family units, are often raised by surrogate parents, have extensive juvenile records and/or foster home placements, have had frequent contact with mental health professionals, and are usually remembered by school teachers and administrators.

b. Extensive research and understanding into specific cultural factors that may have influenced the personality development of the defendant. This is particularly important if the defendant has origins in cultures whose values are significantly different from those represented by the criminal justice system.

9) This information is essential for defense counsel in order to gain detailed, accurate knowledge of the defendant.

10) Such knowledge enables the defense counsel to formulate defense strategies both for the trial and mitigation phases, and to provide the trier of facts with an accurate and detailed understanding of the defendant, his or her environment, culture, and potentially mitigating factors.

11) As stated previously, the process of gathering this information often takes many months and requires the coordination of criminal and social investigators, mental health professionals, and attorneys.

12) The responsibility ultimately lies with the defense attorney to initiate and coordinate this process and provide direction and integration to the defense.

13) To summarize, any preparation for the mitigation phase should include the following:

    I. Obtaining the following background information

        a. The defendant's developmental experiences

        b. The defendant's family dynamics

    c. The parenting capacities in the family of the defendant

    d. The defendant's academic capacities and achievements

    e. The defendant's work experiences, including relationships with coworkers as well as job skills

    f. The defendant's interpersonal relationships and social adjustments

    g. The defendant's sexual and marital history

    h. The defendant's medical history

    i. The psychological functioning across the defendant's lifetime

  II. This information can only be obtained by lengthy interviews with

    a. Family members

    b. Neighbors

    c. Employers

    d. Teachers

    e. Significant people in the defendant's life

    f. Medical and psychiatric professionals

    g. Any other professionals who might be able to provide valuable information given a defendant's particular circumstances

14) In the case of William Green, I have reviewed extensive materials including the following records:

    a. Indiana Boys School

    b. Newspaper articles dated 4/1/70, 5/27/70, and 5/31/72 concerning resident mistreatment at the Indiana Boys School (while William Green was a resident)

    c. Indianapolis Police Department

    d. Tennessee Department of Corrections

    e. Darby County Psychodiagnostic Clinic

    f. Lexington Police Department

    g. Indianapolis Public Schools

    h. Akron Police Department

    i. Centry-Metatech Industries

    j. Western State Hospital, Indianapolis

    k. Mental health records from Darby County Jail

    l. Transcripts of mitigation testimony

15) In addition, I personally interviewed and evaluated William Green on August 25 and September 29, 1989, at the Southern Ohio Correctional Facility. In addition to the interview, I administered psychological tests including the Minnesota Multiphasic Personality Inventory (MMPI), Wechsler Adult Intelligence Scale-Revised (WAIS-R), and the Rorschach Inkblot Test. I also took into consideration the social investigation performed by Richard Ruff and David Brooks, mitigation specialists. That investigation included interviews with 10 brothers and sisters of the defendant, 2 cousins, 2 sisters-in-law, 1 brother-in-law, and a paternal aunt.

UPON MY REVIEW OF THE ABOVE-MENTIONED INFORMATION, I HAVE THE FOLLOWING OPINION:

16) Defense counsel's presentation of mitigation excluded many relevant psychological, social, emotional, and environmental issues in the defendant's life. However, based on my experience of over 40 capital cases, it would not have been possible for defense counsel (with or without the help of a psychologist and social worker with mitigation training) to prepare for mitigation given both the short time and the failure to begin collection of data until after the factfinding phase. The following is a list of those areas where defense counsel fell short of adequate preparation for mitigation:

a. Virtually no interviews occurred with relevant family members who knew William. Little, if any, attempt was made to contact his sister, brothers, aunts, and uncles.

b. Although available, no school records were obtained. These records included complete psychological and intellectual assessments of the defendant during his school years.

c. Because of this lack of investigation, the defense counsel had no clear or in-depth understanding of the defendant, his psychological profile, his environment, or of his offense. Thus, defense counsel had no well formulated, coherent theory of mitigation.

d. No mental health experts were called to testify as to the strengths and weaknesses of the defendant in order to give the jury a total perspective of the crime and the defendant's life circumstances. The psychological evaluation addressed only the issue of ORC § 2929.04 B 3, whether at the time of committing the offense the offender, because of a mental disease or defect, lacked substantial capacity to appreciate the criminality of his conduct or to conform his conduct to the requirements of the law. The evaluator did not take into consideration any of the material listed above which were available for review (with obvious exception of the mitigation transcripts).

e. Therefore, no one was called who could testify as to the defendant's personality developmental or social and emotional history.

f. A psychologist could have presented a more complete picture for the jury during mitigation and could have provided an opportunity for the jury to deliberate about the defendant's strengths and weaknesses. Without such information, no deliberation on these issues was possible.

g. These deficiencies resulted in an inability by the defense to provide the trier of fact with an in-depth understanding of the defendant and his offense to weigh against the aggravating factors presented at the trial.

h. For the reasons cited above and for those which follow, the defendant was deprived any kind of coherent or meaningful defense in his mitigation hearing.

17) Available information reveals considerable and significant data relevant to the issue of balancing the aggravating facts of the crime against mitigating circumstances. This information could have been testified to at mitigation and could have provided a much more thorough understanding of the defendant and the offense.

REVIEW OF AVAILABLE RECORDS, INTERVIEWS, AND EVALUATIONS TO DATE HAS RESULTED IN THE FOLLOWING INFORMATION:

18) William Green is presently a 34-year-old African American male. He is the eighth of 15 children born to Clyde Green and Virginia Riggs Green (both deceased prior to the trial). Clyde was 17, and Virginia 13 at the time of their marriage. Though they grew up in Tennessee, William's parents moved to Indianapolis so Clyde could find better employment. The older children stayed in Tennessee while the younger ones accompanied their parents. Both Clyde and Virginia had addiction problems with alcohol and gambling. These behaviors were in marked contrast to their parents' strong Christian beliefs. In the early years of their marriage, Clyde and Virginia managed fairly well though Clyde was arrested for bad checks and returned to Tennessee for a month.

As Clyde and Virginia continued to drink to excess, they also became much less responsible for paying bills. They then frequently moved to avoid paying rent. Relatives report that Virginia would fail to come home following her drinking binges leaving the 15 children unattended or in the care of the older siblings.

Several traumatic events affected the early development of William. The first serious incident occurred on October 9, 1965. Four young men came to the Green house to see Betty (the fifth oldest child, then aged 15). Clyde refused to let the boys see her (she was too young to be dating) and the men forced their way into the house and attacked Clyde, who managed to cut one of them with a small pocketknife. About a half hour later the four returned with two more of their friends and attacked Clyde, who then ran. The gang followed and cornered Clyde, knocked him to the ground, and beat him to death. This was witnessed by their 10-year-old son, William Green. Clyde died with a blood alcohol level of 0.30%. This remains a vivid memory for William, who spent his early years clinging to his mom and dad.

Following this incident, the family deteriorated, and the children were eventually placed in foster homes or sent to live with relatives. William was sent to a foster home in the Indianapolis area, where he was beaten with a cord for wetting his bed, skipping school, and misbehaving. He ran away from this home and went back to his mother, who was living in the Gordon Home Projects of Indianapolis. She was often drunk and unstable. William was sent to Tennessee, but he presented behavior problems and was soon sent back to Indiana. The children were left alone most of the time and raised themselves. Those who stayed or returned to Tennessee maintained ties with a strong Southern Christian heritage without getting into any legal difficulties. Those who remained in Indiana have had significant problems in adjustment.

In the fall of 1968, William was convicted of shooting his cousin. The incident itself speaks to his adjustment problems, anger, and confusion. William wanted money from his cousin to give for church. When she refused to give him the money, he shot her. He then went to church as if nothing had happened. He was sent to the Indiana Boys School outside Indianapolis. He was there from January of 1969 through December of 1972. It was during this time period that an investigation of the Indiana Boys School revealed abuse, mistreatment, large bruises on the children, shaved heads, and "group" punishment. These abuses were reported in *The Indianapolis News* and the *Christian Science Monitor*. While he was a resident at the school, his mother was killed in a car crash in December of 1969 in Akron, Ohio. William was not informed of her death until he was released in October of 1970. His behavior quickly deteriorated, and he began drinking. This played a part in his reincarceration at the Indiana Boy's School from January 1971 until December 1972.

William's first 15 years were influenced by a number of traumatic events. First of all, he was raised in a family of some 15 children, generally unsupervised by responsible adults. William showed a number of adjustment problems including bed wetting until he was 10 years old. Second, both of his parents exhibited addiction problems with alcohol and gambling. Third, William was a witness to the violent beating death of his father. Fourth, William's family unit deteriorated following his father's death and he was sent to foster homes. Fifth, he was sent to the Indiana Boy's "Home" following the conviction for shooting. This home was investigated for abuse, violence, and corruption during the time period that he was a resident. Finally, his mother was killed in a car crash and William was not told of this until a year later when he was released from the school. The combination of these events left William bereaved, angry, sullen, withdrawn, isolated, and untrusting. He felt as though he had no one left in the world. He then started drinking and engaging in a variety of antisocial behaviors.

As a teenager and young adult, William began to rely on his survival skills, including robbery and burglary. His alcoholism developed unchecked into a serious addiction (not unusual considering that he was the child of an alcoholic). He was, in fact, arrested for public drunkenness on several occasions. He had few friends and only one serious relationship resulting in marriage, to a 16-year-old girl, in 1984. This marriage ended in a divorce in 1985. He remained alienated and isolated for most of his adult life.

Psychological testing based on the Wechsler Adult Intelligence Scale-Revised (WAIS-R) indicates that William Green is functioning in the borderline range of intelligence with a verbal IQ of 76, a performance IQ of 72, giving a full scale IQ of 73. This places him at approximately the third percentile. These scores can be compared to previous intellectual assessments dating back to 1961 with a reported IQ of 62 (placing him in the mental retarded range at age 6), IQ of 70 in 1964, IQ of 68 in 1965, and IQ of 77 in 1967. The Psychodiagnostic Clinic reported a full scale IQ of 74. In summary, William Green's intellectual ability is within the IQ range of 65 to 75. School records indicate poor intellectual ability, and he was held in the fourth grade for 2 years (1964-1966).

William was administered the Minnesota Multiphasic Personality Inventory (MMPI) and the Rorschach Inkblot Test. On the MMPI, William appears to have responded to the test with sincerity and a normal degree of expressiveness. His profile suggests that he is depressed with accompanying feelings of helplessness and hopelessness. On the one hand, this may not be surprising considering his current status. However, his scores are significantly more elevated than other death row inmates I have evaluated, and his responses reveal a life-long sense of depression, feelings of inadequacy, alienation, and family problems. My opinion is that this is a man who has been depressed most of his life and resorted to alcohol to combat these feelings.

On the Rorschach Inkblot Test, William's responses are few in number (12), flat in affect, and consistent with a diagnosis of depression.

In my opinion, William Green is suffering from the following disorders:

Axis I.   Dysthymic Disorder 300.40

              Alcohol Dependence, in remission 303.90

              Borderline Intellectual Functioning, V62.89

Axis II.   Personality Disorder Not Otherwise Specified

              With Dependent and Antisocial Features, 301.90

The above diagnoses are based on a review of all of the available records to date, my psychological evaluation of William Green, and the psychological evaluation and testing performed by the Darby County Psychodiagnostic Clinic.

It is my opinion, with reasonable psychological certainty, that William Green was extremely dependent on both his mother and father. Relatives report that he used to cling to his mother all of the time and that she praised him when he would steal small objects. He appears to have suffered a serious depression following his father's death, resulting in feelings of anger and denial.

He was unable to deal with those feelings and projected much of the blame for his condition on those closest to him, thus alienating much of his family. When his mother died, William's world fell apart and he no longer gave much consideration to the consequences of his behavior. His alcoholism contributed to antisocial conduct, though his borderline intellectual ability also was a contributing factor. The underlying condition for these behaviors, in my opinion, was the depression he suffered though he received no treatment of any kind.

Based on all of the records and accompanying affidavits, it appears that William was constantly exposed to alcoholism and neglect with occasional beatings from foster parents. He learned to cope with basic survival tendencies. He had little responsible adult supervision. Those who were in charge (either in the home or in the Indiana Boys School) were themselves found to be ineffective, irresponsible, and ill-equipped to handle children.

Though he presents many behaviors typical of an antisocial personality, it is my opinion, with reasonable scientific certainty, that these behaviors resulted from the tragic circumstances of his life and his own feeling of abandonment by those closest to him. To this day, he feels abandoned not only by his parents but by his 14 siblings and other relatives. He has few friends, few long-term relationships, and remains alienated and isolated from the world around him.

19) It is my opinion, with reasonable scientific certainty, that the alcoholism, neglect, and tragedies in the life of William Green were a contributing factor to his depression, alcoholism, and personality disorders. These factors should have been presented to the trier of fact and would have been considered as a mitigating factor under Section (B) (7) of the ORC 2929.04.

20) It is my opinion, with reasonable scientific certainty, that William Green's mixed personality disorder with dependent and antisocial features should have been considered as a relevant mitigating factor under Section (B) (7) of the ORC 2929.04.

21) It is my opinion, with reasonable scientific certainty, that William Green's borderline intellectual functioning should have been considered as a relevant mitigating factor under Section (B) (7) of the ORC 2929.04.

22) It is my opinion that all of the information provided in this affidavit could be testified to in a mitigation hearing and that such information could be of consequence to a trier of fact in weighing the aggravating and mitigating factors in this crime.

FURTHER AFFIANT SAYETH NAUGHT.

Chapter 9

SPECIAL ISSUES: COMPETENCY, SANITY, AND THE DEATH PENALTY

A capitally charged defendant, like other criminal defendants, is presumed competent to stand trial unless it can be proved, usually by a preponderance of the evidence, that the defendant lacks sufficient present ability to consult with his or her attorney with a reasonable degree of rational understanding and whether he or she has a rational as well as factual understanding of the proceedings against him or her (see *Dusky v. United States*). The issue of competency to stand trial can be raised by any officer of the court when there is a *bona fide* doubt about the defendant's competence (see *Pate v. Robinson*). However, for strategic reasons, defense attorneys may be reluctant to raise this issue in death penalty cases. Following *Estelle v. Smith*, an evaluation of a capital defendant (who has been properly *Mirandized* by the forensic evaluator) for the sole purpose of competency to stand trial may be subject to testimony at sentencing where future dangerousness is an issue. In all such evaluations, defendants must be represented by counsel and informed of the purposes of the evaluation. The evaluation should focus solely on the pretrial issue and not extend into other areas (mitigation, risk assessment, etc.). In some jurisdictions, the information obtained from this type of evaluation (competency to stand trial) is limited only to the referral issue. Normally, such an evaluation requested by defense counsel may remain under attorney-client privilege unless the expert is called as a witness. Therefore, a referral for competency to stand trial may undermine the defense strategy by supplying to the prosecution information that it could later use to bolster the state's case at sentencing. In most states, the trial court judge decides the issue of competency. In Texas, however, the issue of competency is decided by a jury.

Competency to stand trial is only one among several types of "competencies" that can be raised as an issue in capital cases. "Competence," defined broadly in legal terms but requiring a nuanced inquiry by the consulting mental health professional, may also be raised if the defendant wishes to represent himself or herself (*Godinez v. Moran*), if the defendant wants to waive a jury trial, if the defendant wishes to enter a plea, or if the defendant wants to waive any further appeals, thus expediting his or her own progress toward a possible execution. In *Godinez v. Moran* the Court ruled, among other things, that the standard for measuring a criminal defendant's competency to plead guilty or waive the right to counsel is not higher than, or different from, the "rational understanding" prong of the competency to stand trial standard. The Court has also ruled, however, that defendants must be competent to be executed. To state the obvious, that particular kind of competency evaluation has profound implications.

COMPETENCY TO WAIVE APPEALS

Life on death row can be excruciatingly painful psychologically, emotionally, and physically. Because of mental illness, depression, guilt, social isolation, hopelessness, or the intolerable conditions on death row, a number of inmates prefer that this lengthy process come to an end by waiving any further appeals. These inmate "volunteers" would then give up their right to appeal only if it is determined that they are competent to make that decision. The waiver must be knowing, intelligent, and voluntary, and ultimately an evaluation may be requested in order to determine that the inmate is competent to waive the appeals and also, therefore, competent to be executed. The decision to give up on the appellate process may be part of a conscious or unconscious suicide attempt or a reflection of the chronic deprivation suffered while on death row making "death" preferable to life (Cunningham, in press). It is a difficult task evaluating these "volunteers" because they generally have some understanding that their attorneys seek to find them "incompetent," which places them into some kind of legal limbo until that issue is resolved. It is, therefore, important to review all available inmate records in order to document the course of the inmate's progression towards the decision to end appeals. Most inmates do not give up their right to appeal until they have spent years on death row. The institution would normally have numerous evaluations over that period of time. In any event, the evaluation must address the key areas of "knowing," "intelligent," and "voluntary." As the case history below demonstrates, even a mentally ill inmate can be found competent to waive appeals.

COMPETENCY TO BE EXECUTED

The Supreme Court established in *Rees v. Peyton* that prior to execution a defendant must have the "capacity to appreciate his position and make a rational choice with respect to continuing or abandoning further litigation or on the other hand whether he is suffering from a mental disease, disorder, or defect which may substantially affect his capacity." The court further clarified its ruling in the landmark case of *Ford v. Wainwright*, establishing that the Eighth Amendment prohibits execution of the "insane." In his concurring opinion Justice Powell wrote,

> Whether a convict is competent to be executed for Eighth Amendment purposes turns solely on whether the convict is aware of his impending execution and the reasons for it. If the defendant perceives the connection between his crime and his punishment, the retributive goal of the criminal law is satisfied. And only if the defendant is aware that his death is approaching can he prepare himself for his passing. Accordingly, I would hold that the Eighth Amendment forbids the execution only of those who are unaware of the punishment they are about to suffer and why they are to suffer it. (477 U.S. 399 at 2608)

The Court, however, has provided little in the way of guidelines for evaluating defendants' competency to be executed. An inmate may "understand" the punishment that he or she is about to receive, but that may not suggest an "appreciation" of the various events that have led to this moment. Given the inherent ambiguity of the *Ford* decision, the evaluator should offer a descriptive rather than conclusionary report that describes the perceptions and relevant preparations of the offender. The evaluation should include the inmate's own statements regarding his or her understanding of the execution and his or her expectations of the likely outcome. The evaluation should address the inmate's understanding of the reasons that he or she is being executed as well as a third-party observation of that understanding (corrections officers, ministers, family, etc.).

A number of ethical issues resulting from the *Ford* decision have been raised by Heilbrun (1987). He proposed five practical suggestions. First, he stated that the evaluators should be skilled in the clinical-legal area and chosen in a manner to avoid bias. Second, evaluators have an ethical obligation to inform the inmate of the nature and purpose of the evaluation. Third, the evaluation should be comprehensive including an assessment of intellectual functioning, personality characteristics, pathology, and malingering. Fourth, the evaluation should take into consideration the physical environment and daily routine for the inmate. Finally, a written report should include all sources of information and documentation. Given the particularly serious nature of these evaluations, Zapf, Boccaccini, and Brodsky (2003) have recommended minimum standards for competency to be executed evaluations in addition to the Specialty Guidelines for Forensic Psychologists (1991). They proposed an interview checklist for evaluations of competency for execution. The checklist would include the following four areas for assessment: (a) an understanding of the reasons for punishment, (b) an understanding of the punishment, (c) an ability to appreciate and reason beyond simple factual understanding, and (d) an ability to assist defense counsel. Though relatively few such evaluations are actually performed, the stakes are obviously high. Psychologists or psychiatrists who perform these evaluations need to exercise special caution before concluding that they are adequately prepared, both professionally and personally, for their unique demands. (For an example of a competency to be executed report, see Heilbrun, Marczyk, & DeMatteo, 2002, Chapter 6.)

CRIMINAL RESPONSIBILITY AND THE DEATH PENALTY

Criminal responsibility is not a typical defense strategy in any criminal trial including capital trials. Though high publicity cases have significant media coverage for such a plea (consider the case of the Washington, DC area sniper, Lee Malvo), the actual use of an "insanity" plea is estimated to be 1% (Silver, Cirincione, & Steadman, 1994). Most states have a standard predicated on *McNaughten*. In what is often referred to as the *McNaughten Rule*, defendants are not responsible for criminal conduct if it can be clearly proved that, at the time of committing the act, those accused were laboring under such a defect of reason, from disease of the mind, as not to know the nature and quality of the act they were doing, or, if they did know it, that they did not know what they were doing was wrong (taken from Wrightsman, Nietzel, & Fortune, 1998). Many states followed the recommendations from the Model Penal Code (adopted in *United States v. Brawner*). As a result, in order to be found insane, a defendant, as a result of mental disease or defect, must not possess substantial capacity to appreciate the criminality of his or her conduct. Most states have eliminated the so-called volitional prong of the *Brawner* test which reads, "or to conform his conduct to the requirements of the law." Each state that retains an "insanity defense" has its own version of the language for "insanity." However, five states have eliminated the defense altogether (Colorado, Idaho, Kansas, Montana, and Utah).

The issue of criminal responsibility ("sanity" at the time of the act) is normally raised during the trial in chief — the factfinding phase. However, regardless of whether the defense has pursued a trial-level strategy based on a claim of "insanity," the issue of mental illness can be raised as a mitigating factor. Most states have language in their mitigation statute that is similar to the Model Penal Code "insanity" language. The defendant (who would now be "the offender" since he or she has already been found guilty) can raise the issue at mitigation of "whether, at the time of committing the offense, the offender, because of a mental disease or defect, lacked substantial capacity to appreciate the criminality of the offender's conduct or to conform the offender's conduct to the requirements of the law." This language is *not* meant to re-open at mitigation the issue of criminal responsibility but rather to address the issue of the offender's moral culpability. Even so, this mitigation strategy warrants careful consideration by defense counsel in part because it has the potential to confuse members of the jury. If the jury has already rejected the insanity plea during trial, it may be more inclined to reject mental illness as a mitigating factor at sentencing.

In contrast with cases involving mental retardation, it is not currently unconstitutional to execute the mentally ill. Consider the case of Andrea Yates, the Texas mother who was accused and convicted of killing her five children. Although the jury rejected her insanity plea, it decided against the death penalty, in part because they felt that her mental illness was a mitigating factor. Texas law does not identify specific mitigating factors (such as mental illness), but it does allow for consideration "whether, taking into consideration all of the evidence, including the circumstances of the offense, the defendant's character and background, and the personal moral culpability of the defendant, there is a sufficient mitigating circumstance or circumstances to warrant that a sentence of life imprisonment rather than a death sentence be imposed."

CASE EXAMPLE: COMPETENCY TO BE EXECUTED IN A DEATH ROW "VOLUNTEER"

State of Ohio v. Berry

In December of 1989, Anthony Lozar and Wilford Berry shot and killed Charles J. Mitroff, Jr., while attempting to rob his bakery. Berry had briefly worked there. Berry later stated that he began planning to kill Mitroff about 10 hours before the murder. He purchased an assault rifle and a .22 caliber rifle, and then hid them in an alley next to the bakery entrance. After Mitroff left to begin making deliveries, Berry let Lozar into the bakery. When Mitroff returned, Lozar fired the assault rifle, striking Mitroff in the chest. Mitroff fell to the floor bleeding. He asked for help from Berry, who then shot Mitroff in the head with the .22 caliber rifle. Berry eventually stated that he knew Mitroff was dying after the first shot but believed that one more shot would kill him. Berry and Lozar cleaned the bakery floor and put Mitroff's body into the bakery's van. Subsequently, they drove to Lozar's sister's house and obtained a shovel. Before burying the body under a bridge near downtown Cleveland, Ohio, they removed the victim's wallet. They then drove to a car wash and cleaned the van. Later, they purchased black spray paint, painted the van, and then drove to Kentucky, where they were eventually apprehended (see *State v. Berry*, 1993 Ohio App. LEXIS 5101). A possible motive for the crime was provided by Berry's sister, who reported that Mr. Mitroff had almost hit her and her son with his van not long before Berry's employment at the bakery.

Anthony Lozar, who was tried first, waived his right to a jury trial and had his case heard by a three-judge panel. He was convicted of aggravated murder. The panel rejected the death penalty and gave him instead a sentence of life in prison with parole eligibility after 30 full years. Wilford Berry presented his case to a jury and was convicted of aggravated murder. At the mitigation hearing, the jury heard from a defense psychologist who testified that Berry suffered from "considerable emotional disturbance" and a "psychotic disorder not otherwise specified," as well as a "personality disorder mixed with schizotypal, borderline, and antisocial features" (99 Ohio St. 3rd, 1995, p. 11). The jury was also told of Berry's highly dysfunctional social history, his sexual molestation by babysitters, and the fact that he was the victim of several prison rapes. However, Berry himself requested that the jury hand down a sentence of death rather than a sentence of 20 or 30 years to life. Specifically, it was reported that he looked at the jury of 12 women and stated, "If you let me out I will kill again, probably one of you." The jury decided in favor of death, and the judge imposed that sentence.

Following his conviction and death sentence, Berry then attempted to halt any further proceedings and demanded that the state execute him. It was then that the court ordered him evaluated for his competency to be executed, as well as his competency to waive any further proceedings. It was defense counsel's position that Berry was not competent due to his "schizotypal personality disorder," his "rigid thought process," his tendency toward "extreme isolation and withdrawal," and his tendency to experience psychotic episodes under stress.

The court-appointed psychiatrists, who testified for the state, diagnosed Berry with a "mixed personality disorder with schizotypal, borderline, and antisocial features." The psychiatrists concluded that Berry was competent to decide against pursuing any further legal remedies, using a legal standard that had been established by the court. None of the three experts found Berry to be psychotic. Berry believed that when he died, he would be judged by God and go either to heaven or to hell. The psychiatrists did not regard this sort of commonly held religious belief as a sign of mental illness. Berry had no unusual or delusional beliefs about the afterlife. He considered donating his organs. He understood not only the difference between life and death but the permanence of death.

Berry told all of the evaluating doctors that he would prefer release from imprisonment to death if he thought that this release was a reasonable possibility. The defense psychologist believed that he was being truthful about that, even though she also believed that Berry had a compulsive desire to be dead. Given the evidence, it seemed clear that Berry understood the difference between life and death.

The Public Defenders' chief contention at the evidentiary hearing was that due to his mental disorder, Berry did not *fully* comprehend the ramifications of his decision. Although he clearly understood that abandoning his legal remedies would lead to his death, he did not understand, or so his attorneys argued, that pursuing them could ultimately lead to release from prison, which he said he would prefer to death. This lack of understanding, according to the defense psychologist, resulted from the rigid thinking that was caused by his mental disorder. Having formed the fixed notion that he had little chance of release, Berry refused to listen to his attorneys when they tried to tell him otherwise. At that point in time, Berry sent the following letter (quoted verbatim) to the Chief Justice of the Ohio Supreme Court (copy provided by the presiding trial judge):

Look Here Fuck Face, here it is, another week pass and still you's
[sic] at the Ohio Supreme Court of Appeals are still playing games.
I know that you's are old, But Dam! I didn't think your mind was that
darn slow to the point that it's taken you's this long to think about
my appeals. So why don't you come on down to Mansfield (*location
of Ohio's Death Row*) and see me and I'm pretty sure that after they
buried you, they who are left on the Ohio Supreme Court of Appeals
won't waist [sic] any time on coming back with a decision of turning
down my appeals. You know the appeal I'm talking about? Death
Row Appeals, Case Number 93-2592. So stop letting the rest of the
Judges fuck you and give me my answer to my appeals cause I'm
getting tier [sic] of waiting. You've had a whole month to think about
it. I'll be writing you up next week if I don't have an answer to my
appeals. OK. Fuck Face and to show I mean what I said in this letter
I had it notarized. I want his letter added to my file. Thank you for
your time.

Respectfully submitted,

Wilford Lee Berry, Jr.

The court used the following standard, "A capital defendant is mentally competent to abandon any and all challenges to his death sentence if he has the mental capacity to understand the choice between
life and death and to make a knowing and intelligent decision not to
pursue further remedies. The defendant must fully comprehend the
ramifications of his decision, and must possess the 'ability to reason
logically, i.e., to choose means which relate logically to his ends' " (*State
v. Berry*, 80 Ohio St. 3rd 371).

The reasoning that formed the basis for the court's decision has its
roots in the following language, which can be found in Ohio's Revised
Criminal Code: "The test of whether a convict awaiting execution is
'insane' . . . is not whether he is 'mentally ill,' but whether he has sufficient intelligence to understand the nature of the proceedings against
him, what he was tried for, the purpose of his punishment, the im-
pending fate that awaits him, a sufficient understanding to know any
fact which might exist which would make his punishment unjust or
unlawful, and the intelligence to convey such information to his attorney or the court" (Ohio Revised Code Annotated, § 2949.28, Footnote
7).

The court found Berry competent to waive any further appeals, and,
subsequently he became the first Ohio inmate to be executed in the post-
Furman era. He chose a path that was, in many respects, similar to the
path that had been chosen more than 20 years earlier (1976) by Gary
Gilmore, who had been sentenced to death by a Utah Court. Although
Gilmore, too, ended up being executed, it is difficult not to be struck by

the very different tone he used to have his death sentence carried out. In contrast to Berry's letter to the court, Gary Gilmore sent the following letter to the citizens of Utah while pursuing his execution:

> Don't the people of Utah have courage of their convictions? You sentence a man to die . . . and when I accept this most extreme punishment with grace and dignity, you, the people of Utah want to back down and argue with me about it.
>
> You're silly.
>
> Look, I am sane, rational and more intelligent than the average person.
>
> I've been sentenced to die. I accept that. Let's do it and to hell with all the bullshit.
>
> Most sincerely,
>
> Gary Gilmore
>
> (Cited in 54 S. Cal. L. Rev. 575 at 631)

Chapter 10

MENTAL RETARDATION AND THE DEATH PENALTY

THE SUPREME COURT AND MENTAL RETARDATION

Experts estimate that approximately 10% of inmates on death row are mentally retarded (cited in *Atkins v. Virginia*). Yet, as stated earlier (see Chapter 3), in 2002 the Supreme Court held that executing those with mental retardation violated the Eighth Amendment's ban on cruel and unusual punishment (*Atkins v. Virginia*). Justice Stevens, in his opinion for the Court, stated that "Because of their disabilities in areas of reasoning, judgment, and control of their impulses, however, they do not act with the level of moral culpability that characterizes the most serious adult criminal conduct." In spite of their mental retardation, these defendants were found competent to stand trial and criminally responsible. They could, therefore, be punished to the full extent of law with the exception of the death penalty. The Supreme Court's discussion of mental retardation and the death penalty started 13 years before *Atkins* in *Penry v. Lynaugh*.

In the *Penry* case, the Court held that executing persons with mental retardation was not a violation of the Eighth Amendment because "At the present time there is insufficient evidence of a national consensus against executing the mentally retarded convicted of capital offenses." At the time of *Penry*, only two states prohibited such executions. Since then, 16 more states and the federal government have enacted laws prohibiting the execution of the mentally retarded. The Court then accepted the *Atkins* case:

> Daryl Renard Atkins, was convicted of abduction, armed robbery, and capital murder, and sentenced to death. At approximately midnight on August 16, 1996, Atkins and William Jones, armed with a

semiautomatic handgun, abducted Eric Nesbitt, robbed him, drove him to an automated teller machine in his pickup truck where cameras recorded their withdrawal of additional cash, then took him to an isolated location where he was shot eight times and killed.

The Court's decision to reconsider executing the mentally retarded in light of *Atkins* was based, in part, on a significant number of states that concluded that death is not a suitable punishment for a mentally retarded criminal. The Court stated that "It is not so much the number of these states that is significant, but the consistency of the direction of change. The large number of states prohibiting the execution of mentally retarded persons (and the complete absence of legislation reinstating such executions) provides powerful evidence that today society views mentally retarded offenders as categorically less culpable than the average criminal." The Court recognized that those mentally retarded defendants affected by this opinion (such as Daryl Atkins) "frequently know the difference between right and wrong and are competent to stand trial, but, by definition, have diminished capacities to understand and process information, to communicate, to abstract from mistakes and learn from experience, to engage in logical reasoning, to control impulses, and to understand others' reactions. Their deficiencies do not warrant an exemption from criminal sanctions, but diminish their personal culpability." The Court went on to conclude that executing the mentally retarded did not satisfy either the retributive or the deterrent effect of capital crimes. With regard to retribution, the Court noted that the severity of punishment depends on the offender's culpability. The culpability of an "average mentally retarded offender is insufficient to justify the imposition of death." With regard to deterrence, the Court stated that "the same cognitive and behavioral impairments that make mentally retarded defendants less morally culpable also make it less likely that they can process the information of the possibility of execution as a penalty and, as a result, control their conduct based upon that information." The Court was also concerned that mentally retarded defendants faced a special risk of wrongful execution since they are more likely to confess to crimes that they did not commit.

The decision in *Atkins* clearly states that mentally retarded defendants shall not be executed. However, the decision also grants the states the right to adopt their own standard and criteria for mental retardation. In fact, as of 2004, the State of Virginia is still pursuing the execution of Daryl Atkins, and a hearing has been scheduled to determine if he is mentally retarded under the *Atkins* criteria. In other words, does "*Atkins*" apply to Atkins?

STANDARDS FOR
MENTAL RETARDATION

The American Association on Mental Retardation (AAMR) defines mental retardation as a disability characterized by significant limitations both in intellectual functioning and in adaptive behavior as expressed in conceptual, social, and practical adaptive skills. This disability originates before age 18. The AAMR lists five assumptions essential to the application of the definition. These would also be essential for a forensic evaluation:

1) Limitations in present functioning must be considered within the context of community environments typical of the individual's age, peers, and culture;

2) valid assessment considers cultural and linguistic diversity as well as differences in communication, sensory, motor, and behavioral factors;

3) within an individual, limitations often coexist with strengths;

4) an important purpose of describing limitations is to develop a profile of needed supports; and

5) with appropriate personalized supports over a sustained period, the life functioning of the person with mental retardation generally will improve. (American Association on Mental Retardation, 2002)

The American Psychiatric Association (2000) defines mental retardation as follows:

> The essential feature of Mental Retardation is significantly subaverage general intellectual functioning (Criterion A) that is accompanied by significant limitations in adaptive functioning in at least two of the following skill areas: community resources, self-direction, functional academic skills, work, leisure, health, and safety (Criteria B). The onset must occur before age 18 years (Criterion C). . . . Significantly subaverage intellectual functioning is defined as an IQ of about 70 or below. . . . It should be noted that there is a measurement of error of approximately 5 points in assessing IQ, although this may vary from instrument to instrument (e.g., a Wechsler IQ of 70 is considered to represent a range of 65-75). Thus, it is possible to diagnose Mental Retardation in individuals with IQs between 70 and 75 who exhibit significant deficits in adaptive functioning. Conversely, Mental Retardation would not be diagnosed in an individual with IQ lower than 70 if there are no significant deficits or impairments in adaptive functioning. (*DSM-IV-TR*, pp. 41-42)

The definition for mental retardation is, therefore, somewhat flexible. Hypothetically, it is possible to diagnose mental retardation in individuals with full scale IQs as high as 75. Likewise, it would be possible to rule out mental retardation in individuals with IQs as low as 65, assuming that there is no impairment in their adaptive behavior.

ASSESSMENT OF INTELLECTUAL FUNCTIONING

Wechsler (1958) defined intelligence as a global concept that involves the ability of an individual to act purposefully, think rationally, and deal effectively with the environment. It can be assumed, therefore, that mentally retarded individuals demonstrate at least some impairment in these areas. In the manuals for both the original Wechsler Adult Intelligence Scale (WAIS; Wechsler, 1955) and the Wechsler Adult Intelligence Scale-Revised (WAIS-R; Wechsler, 1981), mental retardation was defined as anyone scoring a full scale IQ of 69 or below. In the third edition of the Wechsler Adult Intelligence Scale (WAIS-III; Wechsler, 1997), individuals with an IQ of below 70 are classified as "extremely low" rather than the classification of "mentally retarded" or the term "intellectually deficient" used in the Wechsler Intelligence Scale for Children (3rd ed.) (WISC-III; Wechsler, 1991). The change in terminology is intended to avoid the implication that a very low IQ score is sufficient evidence for the classification of "mental retardation" or "intellectually deficient" (WAIS-III Manual, p. 25). However, an individual with a full scale IQ of 70 is presumed to have an IQ that falls between 67 and 75 with a confidence level of 95%. Similarly, an individual with a tested full scale IQ of 75 is presumed to have an IQ that falls between 71 and 80 with a confidence level of 95% (WAIS-III Manual, p. 197). The upper boundary of IQ scores used in the classification of mental retardation is flexible to reflect the statistical variance inherent in all intelligence tests. Simply put, an IQ test is no longer sufficient for diagnosing mental retardation.

THE FLYNN EFFECT

Over time, individual IQ scores have been rising (the Flynn Effect) ranging from 5 to 25 points thus significantly affecting the diagnosis of mental retardation. Kanaya, Scullin, and Ceci (2003) note that an individual diagnosed with mental retardation at the time that the WAIS-R or Wechsler Intelligence Scale for Children-Revised (WISC-R; Wechsler, 1974) was introduced might later score well within the borderline range of intelligence on those same tests. Thus, they state that individuals might be diagnosed with mental retardation based on the year that they were tested rather than on their cognitive abilities. In other words, they might score in the mentally retarded range of intelligence if tested towards the beginning of the norming cycle for that particular test, and conversely score in the borderline range of intelligence if tested towards the end of the norming cycle. These results could have a significant impact on the assessment of death row inmates or capitally charged defendants since an IQ testing may have been a function of the age of the test itself. Kanaya et al. point out that Daryl Atkins was tested with the WAIS-III the year it was released. Since he scored an IQ of 59, no adaptive functioning assessment would have been required. Had he scored higher than a 59, adaptive functioning would have been assessed as well.

ASSESSMENT OF ADAPTIVE FUNCTIONING

As indicated earlier, the American Association on Mental Retardation defines mental retardation as a significant limitation in intellectual functioning but also in adaptive functioning. The adaptive functioning component requires that the tested intellectual impairment coincide with "real-world" disabling effects. The purpose of this assessment is to determine that the individual is not simply a poor test-taker. Adaptive functioning typically relies on third-party observers including family, friends, teachers, and coworkers when applicable. Third-party contacts should be carefully questioned about the various adaptive behavior arenas.

Several methods have been developed to assess adaptive functioning. The Adaptive Behavior Assessment System (Brown & Leigh, 2000) is the comprehensive, diagnostic assessment of individuals having difficulties with the daily adaptive skills necessary to function effectively in their environments, given the typical demands placed on individuals of the same age. The Adaptive Behavior Inventory evaluates the functional daily living skills of school-age children between the ages of 6 and 18 (Brown & Leigh, 2000). The Adaptive Behavior Scale-Residential and Community (ABS-RC:2) is the 1993 revision of the 1969 and 1974 AAMR Adaptive Behavior Scales and is for adults up to age 80 (Nihira, Leland, & Lambert, 1993). Similarly, the Vineland Adaptive Behavior Scales (Sparrow, Balla, & Cicchetti, 1984 with expected revision in 2005) provide a comprehensive assessment of adaptive behavior that provides a basis for individual educational, habilitative, or treatment plans. As noted previously, adaptive functioning usually takes into account self-direction, functioning academic skills, work, leisure, health, safety, personal hygiene, self-control, and aspects of unmanageable behavior. The diagnosis of mental retardation thus reflects the totality of an individual's psychosocial-cognitive level of functioning and must be based on pre-existing (prior to age 18) evidence of the same.

The burden to investigate mental retardation would normally fall to the defense attorneys, who would then retain psychologists and investigators for this purpose. If the issue of mental retardation is not raised prior to trial, it is one that should be raised during postconviction where there is clear evidence of impaired intellectual functioning. It is not uncommon for defendants with borderline intelligence to fall on either side of the mental retardation spectrum throughout their lives. When mental retardation is suspected in a capitally charged defendant, James Ellis, who represented Atkins to the Supreme Court, has suggested the following statutory language for such defendants:

> If defense counsel has a good faith belief that the defendant in a capital case has mental retardation, counsel shall file a motion with the court, requesting a finding that the defendant is not death-eligible because of mental retardation. Such a motion shall be filed within [time period] after the prosecution files notice of intent to seek the death penalty, unless the information in support of the motion came to counsel's attention at a later date. Upon receipt of such a motion, the trial court shall conduct a hearing for the presentation of evidence regarding the defendant's possible mental retardation. Both the defense and the prosecution shall have the opportunity to present evidence, including expert testimony. After considering the evidence, the court shall find the defendant is not death-eligible if it finds, by a preponderance of the evidence, that the defendant has mental retardation. If the defendant is not death-eligible because of mental retardation, the trial may proceed as a non-capital trial, and, if convicted, the defendant may be sentenced to any penalty available under state law, other than death. If the court finds that defendant is death-eligible, the case may proceed as a capital trial. The jury shall not be informed of the prior proceedings or the judge's findings concerning the defendant's claim of mental retardation. If the capital trial results in a verdict of guilty to a capital charge, the parties shall be entitled to present evidence to the jury on the issue of whether the defendant has mental retardation. Having heard the evidence and arguments, the jury shall be asked to render a special verdict on the issue of mental retardation. The special verdict shall ask the jury to answer the question: "Do you unanimously find, beyond a reasonable doubt, that the defendant does not have mental retardation?" If the jury answers "yes," the case shall proceed to a penalty phase under

[state statute regarding penalty phase of capital trials]. If the jury answers the question "no," defendant may be sentenced to any penalty available under state law, other than death. (See DPIC; Ellis & Luckasson, 1985.)

Chapter 11

ANTISOCIAL PERSONALITY DISORDER, PSYCHOPATHY, AND RISK ASSESSMENT

In 1959, Norman Mailer claimed that we had come to the "hour of the psychopath." He suggested that the criminal and the psychopath had evolved in a new way that made them more adaptable to the demands of late-twentieth century life. Though Mailer produced no empirical evidence in support of this position, there is ample data today to support the thesis that there is an as yet imperfectly understood collusion of sorts between the environment and the autonomic nervous system that allows a certain subset of individuals to engage in antisocial activities undaunted by the probability of reprisals. In addition to a probable physiological predisposition that inclines these individuals toward stimulation-seeking behavior, the antisocial personality often develops in environments where there are inadequate adult role models to encourage the individual's acquisition of a prosocial value system. The antisocial personality seeks immediate gratification just as a child would, often without pausing to consider the impact of his or her actions on other people.

HISTORY OF THE ANTISOCIAL PERSONALITY DISORDER

The antisocial personality has been a subject of investigation dating back to Biblical times. The "stubborn and rebellious son" (see Deuteronomy 21: 18-20) evidently had features that were similar to the antisocial personality. For example, he failed to learn from experience, did not respect authority, and failed to conform to society's standards. In the nineteenth century, Pinel (1962/1806) wrote of individuals who suffered from "*manie sans delire*" or "madness without confusion."

Such individuals appeared to engage in senseless and self-defeating behavior (see Smalldon, 1993). From the eighteenth century through the twentieth century, many terms were used to describe the antisocial personality. A number of early investigators coined their own terms: Rush's "corporeal disease," Pritchard's "moral insanity," Koch's "psychopathic inferiority," and Partridge's "sociopath" (Maughs, 1941). Until recently, there has not been a clear distinction between the characteristics of the antisocial personality and psychopathy.

Modern theories of psychopathy essentially begin with Cleckley's analysis of psychopathic behavior in his classic, *The Mask of Sanity* (first published in 1945 and revised in 1964). According to Cleckley, the psychopath suffers from a "semantic disorder" or what he referred to as "semantic dementia." The psychopath appears to mimic the normal human personality, and wears a "mask of sanity." He (Cleckley referred only to males) exists within a severely restricted range of emotional arousal. One result is that he fails to profit from past experience. In their study of the psychopathic style, Johns and Quay (1962) referred to the psychopath's core deficit as "knowing the words, but not the music." The psychopath understands the denotative meaning of words and actions, but not the emotional flavor and implications.

Recent discussions in the literature have focused on differences between the individuals with antisocial personality disorder and the psychopath, even though these terms are sometimes, and erroneously, used interchangeably. Wallace et al. (2000) argued that psychopathy and antisocial personality disorder should be considered as distinct diagnostic entities. He and his colleagues state that because of an empirically supported information-processing deficiency, psychopathy has more in common with attention-deficit/hyperactivity disorder than with a "personality disorder." Gacono (2000), Hare (1970), and Meloy (1988, 1995) insist that there are significant differences between these two disorders. Young et al. (2000) report that, when compared to the nonpsychopathic antisocial personality, psychopaths have higher IQs, evidence better performance (although still impaired) across all neuropsychological tests, have been more violent in the community, and have more prison disciplinary problems. In addition, when compared to nonpsychopaths, psychopaths (among other findings) were 10 times more likely to have used drugs at a younger age, 10 times more likely not to have an Axis I major mental disorder, 7 times more likely to have histories of severe violence in the community, and 8 times more likely to continue assaultive behavior in prison. Whereas, the antisocial personality disorder tends to run its course by the late twenties, the psychopath (who often begins his or her criminal conduct in early adolescence) exhibits criminal propensities well into his or her fifth decade of life. The psychopath is much more versatile and flexible engaging in a variety of criminal conduct throughout the life span. (See also Eysenck, 1977; Gacono, 2000; Hare 1965, 1970; Lindner, 1944; Meloy, 1992, 1995; and Quay 1965.)

Physiological studies of the antisocial personality disorder have demonstrated lower autonomic arousal as reflected by lower resting heart rate levels and other autonomic indicators (Raine, 1993). The inference that can be drawn from Raine, as well as Mednick (1977), is that lowered autonomic functioning translates into a lack of fear, in fact a deficient understanding of the whole concept of fear, which may result in stimulation-seeking behavior. Thus, these individuals tend not to experience an anticipatory fear response that would normally inhibit antisocial conduct. For example, most of us would jump at the sound of a fire alarm with an accompanying increase in heart rate and autonomic arousal. Research indicates that the physiological response to a fire alarm for at least some of those diagnosed with an antisocial personality disorder is a lower heart rate and lower autonomic arousal.

Research also suggests a likely genetic contribution to the development of the antisocial personality disorder. According to *DSM-IV-TR*, the diagnosis of antisocial personality disorder is more common among first degree biological relatives of individuals with the disorder than it is among members of the general population. One could argue, then, the etiology of the antisocial personality disorder involves the combination of numerous factors, including genetics, neurology, and the environmental/social milieu.

THE ANTISOCIAL PERSONALITY DISORDER AND MITIGATION

Perhaps the most difficult task for a defense attorney in death penalty litigation is trying to marshal "mitigation" for a defendant with antisocial personality disorder (APD) especially if there is a presumption that he or she is a psychopath — as many prosecutors would imply. There are, of course, many other difficult defendants (consider the borderline personality or the paranoid schizophrenic, for example), but the antisocial personality presents a particularly daunting challenge for purposes of mitigation. The diagnosis of antisocial personality disorder has a strong enough negative connotation. A "psychopath" is even worse from the defense perspective.

Having said that, however, I should perhaps add that the antisocial personality (as distinct from the psychopath) may not be as difficult for a jury to understand as other disorders, such as borderline personality disorder, the schizoid personality disorder, or the dissociative disorders. According to the *Diagnostic and Statistical Manual of Mental Disorders* (4ᵗʰ ed. txt. rev.; American Psychiatric Association, 2000), the antisocial personality disorder is characterized by a "pervasive pattern of disregard for, and violation of, the rights of others that begins in childhood or early adolescence and continues into adulthood" (p. 701). The specific diagnostic criteria are as follows:

A. There is a pervasive pattern of disregard for and violation of the rights of others occurring since age 15 years. As indicated by three (or more) of the following:

   (1) failure to conform to social norms with respect to lawful behaviors as indicated by repeatedly performing acts that are grounds for arrest

   (2) deceitfulness, as indicated by repeated lying, use of aliases, or conning others for personal profit or pleasure

   (3) impulsivity or failure to plan ahead

   (4) Irritability and aggressiveness, as indicated by repeated physical fights or assaults

   (5) reckless disregard for safety of self or others

   (6) consistent irresponsibility, as indicated by repeated failure to sustain consistent work behavior or honor financial obligations

   (7) lack of remorse, as indicated by being indifferent to or rationalizing having hurt, mistreated, or stolen from another

B. The individual is at least 18 years.

C. There is evidence of Conduct Disorder with onset before age 15 years.

D. The occurrence of antisocial behavior is not exclusively during the course of Schizophrenia or a Manic Episode. (*DSM-IV-TR*, p. 706)

According to Cunningham and Reidy (1998a) and based on the previous work by Rogers et al. (1994), there are 397,683 different criteria combinations that could result in a diagnosis of antisocial personality disorder. It's no wonder, then, that the estimate of individuals with APD in a prison population ranges from 49% to 80% (Cunningham & Reidy, 2001). This suggests that an antisocial defendant in a capital case might not be all that different from the majority of noncapitally charged prison inmates.

For purposes of this discussion, let us assume that a defendant may well have an antisocial personality disorder but is not a "psychopath."

The role of the psychologist in death penalty litigation often requires testimony about the antisocial personality as well as the APD. There have been a number of publications specific to capital sentencing and the challenges presented by the APD (see, for example, Cunningham & Reidy, 1998a, 1998b, 2001; Meloy, 1988, 1995).

The first task for the psychologist would be to assess the defendant and make an accurate differential diagnosis. Because the APD is a diagnosis based primarily on past conduct rather than on current personality characteristics, there is reason for special caution. And because the diagnosis requires previous evidence of a conduct disorder, in the absence of a prior conduct disorder diagnosis the question needs to be raised whether the defendant may actually have a different problem, perhaps attention-deficit/hyperactivity disorder, an unspecified neurological impairment, or behavior that while deviant to members of the majority culture may actually have been viewed as "normal" by members of the defendant's own cultural group. If the defendant comes from a highly dysfunctional family, as most defendants do, it is possible that early neglect or early trauma, combined with deficient parenting, may have resulted in posttraumatic stress disorder (PTSD), an attachment disorder, or depression.

Though PTSD, or for that matter any variety of other disorders, may be present in addition to the antisocial personality disorder, the psychologist can provide the jury with insight into how and why APD develops. In certain cases, it is possible that a particular defendant, given his or her life circumstances, has a disorder that is relatively easy to understand and explain. And it is fair to say that many individuals with this disorder adapt reasonably well to prison. Antisocial personality disorder does not develop in a vacuum. Early childhood experiences of trauma, neglect, abuse, inconsistent discipline, poor parental role models, parental alienation, poverty, and countless other factors are all relevant to the challenge of explaining the development of the APD. In this sense, the behaviors associated with a diagnosis of APD may have evolved as a means of survival for the young child as he or she struggled to cope with his or her own particular social experiences. For the delinquent, drug dealing and petty crimes often appear to be the industry of opportunity in the only culture that he or she really knows. The adult, given the environment in which he or she was raised, has often incorporated the maladaptive (though perhaps superficially "successful") patterns of behavior that he or she learned as a child. Because these behaviors worked before, why should they not work now? Or so the logic sometimes appears to go.

Of course, none of these factors is presented as a way of "excusing" the conduct of the defendant. They are, however, at least partial explanations of how a young child raised in certain conditions might evolve over time into an antisocial adult. By offering the jury this kind of background information, the psychologist might be able to give the jury some understanding of the overwhelming confusion and fear that a particular child experienced growing up, and of that child's (perhaps unsuccessful) attempts to cope with the reality of his or her day-to-day circumstances. This type of explanation addresses the moral culpability of the defendant at time of sentencing.

RISK ASSESSMENT

There are approximately 22 states that list future dangerousness as a statutory aggravating factor in death penalty litigation. In several states, jurors must answer the question of whether there is a probability that the defendant would, at some point, commit acts of violence that would make him or her a continuing threat to society (see Texas Code 19.03 and Art. 37.071 and Oregon ORS § 163.150, 2001).

Cunningham and Reidy (1998a, 1998b, 2001) have written extensively on this issue and the inherent problems. One concern, expressed by Cunningham (in press), is the "operational definition" of such words as "criminal acts of violence," "probability," and "continuing threat to society." For example, is "probability" perceived to be the same as "possibility"? Are verbal threats to staff, or fights among inmates, representative of acts that members of the majority culture would regard as "constituting a continuing threat to society"? If that were the case, then Cunningham rightly suggests that nearly all inmates would qualify.

This is particularly relevant in capital sentencing because the "society" to which incarcerated inmates (who will be serving a minimum sentence of 40 years) belong is prison, where violence occurs far more frequently than it does outside prison. Simply put, the questions become: What is the probability that a capitally charged defendant who will be serving a life sentence (with parole eligibility after serving 20 years, 30 years, etc.) will engage in future acts of violence? And, is this probability different from what it would be for anyone else serving a life sentence? Edens, Petrila, and Buffington (2001) point out that none of the published research on inmates serving life sentences had examined the relationship between psychopathy and institutional violence. Instruments like the Psychopathy Checklist-Revised (PCL-R; Hare, 2003) would be of little use for any future prediction because most of the PCL-R literature has examined offenders who were returned to the community in their late 20s or early 30s. There is, as Cunningham and Reidy (2001) have pointed out, only a very weak empirical foundation for use in establishing the base rate of institutional violence for these types of offenders. Sorensen and Pilgrim (2000) reported that the rate of homicide among incarcerated murderers in Texas was .2 per 1,000 inmates per year and that after 4-1/2 years in prison, only 1 in 1,000 inmates had committed a homicide.

CASE EXAMPLE:
THE MURDER OF A POLICE OFFICER

On November 17, 1997, Odraye Jones shot and killed police officer William Glover. Glover had responded to a dispatcher with the Ashtabula City Police Department, who had stated that Jones had an outstanding felony warrant and was in the vicinity. Jones had told his cousin a few days before that he had robbed someone and "was going to shoot at the police if they ever tried to arrest him."

Officer Glover responded to the dispatcher's call and spotted Jones with a few of his friends. When he approached, Jones fled on foot. Officer Glover pursued him. Shortly after the pursuit began, Jones turned and fired on Officer Glover. Officer Glover sustained wounds to his face, the top of his head, and his right shoulder. The wounds to his face and head were inflicted from a distance of less than 1 foot. He later died as a result of the shooting. At the time he was shot, his duty weapon was still in its holster, which was snapped shut.

According to testimony at trial, after firing the first shot Jones walked up to Officer Glover and fired several more shots. Officer Glover fell to the ground. Jones then fled, ran to a nearby fence, and began to climb through a hole. At that point he stopped, turned around, and ran back to the wounded officer. It was reported that Jones kicked Officer Glover in the chest, leaving a large visible bruise. Then Jones left the scene.

Shortly after the shooting, another police officer spotted Jones running away. The officer got out of his car and ordered Jones to stop. Jones ignored the command and continued running. The officer pursued Jones to a nearby apartment complex. Jones stopped at the door to an apartment and began trying to force his way inside. While Jones managed to squeeze part of his body through the door, the tenant in the apartment prevented him from fully entering. As Jones was struggling to get through the door, the officer approached Jones, drew his weapon, and ordered Jones to the ground. Jones threw his revolver behind him. It landed in some nearby shrubbery. After the officer had ordered Jones to the ground again, he finally complied. The weapon was quickly recovered and found to match the bullets that had been removed from Officer Glover. Additional cartridges were found in Jones' pocket. Gunshot residue was found on his hands. An eyewitness stated that she saw a man running from the scene who was wearing a Green Bay Packers football jacket (which Jones had, in fact, been wearing).

Jones maintained his innocence throughout all interviews with the defense-retained psychologist and everyone else involved in the case. However, at one point he suggested that his defense attorneys consider a plea of insanity. When told that with an insanity plea he would be asked to discuss the shooting, he declined to pursue that plea. The jury found him guilty of aggravated murder with the death penalty specification of killing a police officer in the line of duty.

Much of Jones' mitigation evidence focused upon his relationship with his mother. In mitigation, the defense presented testimony that he was born to a 16-year-old mother who was unable to care for him. His primary caregiver was his foster grandmother (who had also been the foster parent for Jones' mother). Jones had no relationship with his father. Nor did he have any positive male role models in his life. His natural mother was a drug user who had been in various legal problems due to her substance abuse. When Jones was only 6 years old, his mother was incarcerated for theft. When he was 13, she died from a drug overdose, an apparent suicide. The testimony of several witnesses suggested that the death of his mother was a turning point in his life. He became involved with gangs and was frequently truant from school until he was eventually expelled.

Psychological, neuropsychological, and neurological evaluations found that he met the criteria for diagnosis of antisocial personality disorder, cognitive disorder (not otherwise specified), and cannabis abuse. The antisocial behavior that he engaged in (which the defense explained as an attachment disorder) was shown as having its roots in his highly dysfunctional family, the lack of effective role models in his life, the absence of male bonding, and the enabling behavior engaged in by an equally antisocial and drug dependent mother. His behavior was, in other words, a not unpredictable reflection of his survival instincts, his personality a reflection of the lack of empathy and moral development in his upbringing. His mother was 15 when she became pregnant, 16 when he was born. She was clearly unable to provide adequate parenting, especially given her own drug, alcohol, and legal problems. His foster grandmother was at best inconsistent in terms of her ability to provide for him and the other children in her care, which included his mother. Following his mother's death, Odraye's behavior showed clear signs of deterioration. He joined the local gang and gained a measure of acceptance in that milieu.

As a result of Odraye's early childhood experiences, he bonded to no one, had little capacity for empathy, and had shut off his emotions from the rest of the world. Only under conditions of strict supervision, such as that provided by the Department of Youth Services, had he demonstrated some ability to engage in sustained, goal-directed activity, such as completing his GED.

Testimonial evidence in the record suggested that he clearly had an antisocial personality and suffered from an attachment disorder, which may have created in him an inability to empathize, as well as an ability to rationalize behavior that violated the rights of others. His mitigation evidence suggested that violence and death had characterized much of his life. Both his grandmother and his great-grandmother, for example, had died from gunshot wounds. A close cousin had committed suicide. One of Odraye's daughters had died. In addition to these personal tragedies, an uncle of his was incarcerated for murder. At the age of 16, Jones was severely beaten and robbed by a "friend." The jury was also told of an incident in which Odraye had been severely beaten, robbed, and left in a coma. The mitigation evidence presented was not sufficient for the jury to overcome the aggravating factors. The jury returned a verdict of death and the court imposed the death sentence.

Upon appellate review, the Ohio State Supreme Court ruled as follows:

> Nothing in the nature and circumstances of the offense mitigates Jones's crime. A mere week before he killed Officer Glover, Jones professed to his cousin that he would kill any officer who attempted to arrest him. To this end, Jones armed himself with a .38 caliber revolver and loaded it with hollow point bullets, a particularly deadly form of ammunition. Jones displayed chilling mercilessness in his killing of Officer Glover, firing the fatal shots at point-blank range. He then fled the scene, stopping only to kick the wounded and defenseless officer. Jones surrendered only when all available means of escape had been exhausted. Upon review of the evidence in mitigation, it appears that Jones had a chaotic and troubled childhood. We find that Jones's background and personality disorders are entitled to some weight in mitigation. At the time he committed this offense, Jones was twenty-one years old. Jones's relative youth is entitled to some, but minimal, weight in mitigation. Nothing in the nature and circumstances of the crime is mitigating. We determine that the aggravating circumstances outweigh the mitigating factors presented. In order to escape apprehension for his prior aggravated robbery offense, Jones knowingly killed a police officer who was, at the time, engaged in his professional duties. After considerable thought and review, we conclude that these aggravating circumstances outweigh the mitigating evidence beyond a reasonable doubt. (*State v. Jones*, 2002 Ohio 6914, 2002 Ohio 2074, 2001 Ohio 57)

Chapter 12

CASE STUDY: BOO AND RAIL DO A LICK

Every capital case is different, presenting different challenges for mitigation as well as prosecution. Though the majority of capital defendants come from highly dysfunctional families, that fact is usually not sufficient for purposes of mitigation. Jurors need more than "The defendant had a bad childhood" in order to consider a life sentence as opposed to the death penalty. The task for defense attorneys is to present evidence in such a way as to demonstrate that the defendant is something more than the crimes for which he or she is charged and that the defendant was damaged during his or her formative years, significantly affecting his or her moral development and the resulting choices that he or she made during the period of time prior to arrest. The murder does not tell the whole story of the defendant's life. Though the prosecutor may view the murder as indicative of the defendant's propensity for violence, the defense attorney must demonstrate the unique circumstances of the defendant's life that put him or her in the situation for which a death penalty is a serious possibility. Perhaps Mr. Michael Miller, the former Prosecuting Attorney for Franklin County in Columbus, Ohio, summed it up best in a personal communication: "The defendant is not as good as you (the psychologist) think he is and he is not as bad as I think he is."

The following case presents some of the problems typically encountered in capital litigation. The murder was highly publicized, heinous, and tried in a relatively small community in Ohio. The defendants were African American. The victims were two white college students who had only very brief contact with one of the defendants prior to the murder. As with many cases involving codefendants, often the defense theory of mitigation is to cast aspersion on the codefendant, thereby deflecting some of the horror of the case from its own client.

This was part of the strategy in the present case. The focus for this mitigation is Nathan Herring, known as "Boo."

CASE HISTORY

Aaron Land and Brian Muha were two undergraduates at the Franciscan University of Steubenville in Steubenville, Ohio. According to the University's Website, "The college, inspired by the teaching of St. Francis of Assisi, offers an academic and faith-based educational program that helps students develop their gifts and knowledge while following Jesus Christ, the Way, the Truth, and the Life. The Catholic educational environment prepares students spiritually and intellectually to transform the culture through their future vocations and careers" (University Website). Aaron and Brian rented an apartment a few blocks away from the University.

On May 19, 1999, Nathan "Boo" Herring and Terrell "Rail" Yarbrough, both 19-year-old African American males and small time drug dealers, broke into the Land and Muha apartment with the stated purpose to do a "lick" (a quick burglary/robbery to steal money for drugs). When a third roommate appeared and then escaped, Herring and Yarbrough panicked. Land and Muha were robbed, kidnapped, beaten, driven across two state lines (West Virginia and Pennsylvania), made to perform oral sex, and finally forced to march up a hillside to an isolated area where they were both shot in the head and killed. Herring and Yarbrough then took a credit card from Brian Muha.

Herring and Yarbrough drove to Pittsburgh, Pennsylvania, where Herring was caught on a bank video trying to use Muha's ATM card. While in Pittsburgh, Herring and Yarbrough decided to steal a car and followed a woman (who happened to be a clinical psychologist) driving a BMW. They broke into her home. These events occurred within hours of the murders of Land and Muha. Herring took the BMW and followed Yarbrough back to Steubenville. Fingerprints and blood of Herring were found in both the BMW and in Muha's Chevy Blazer. The defendants were arrested the next day.

Nathan Herring and Terrell Yarbrough were charged in a 20-count indictment. The indictment included two counts of aggravated robbery, each with a firearm specification; one count of aggravated burglary, with a firearm specification; two counts of kidnapping, each with a firearm specification; one count of gross sexual imposition; six counts of aggravated murder for the murder of Land, each with firearm specifications and aggravating circumstances specifications (capital offense); six counts of aggravated murder for the murder of Muha, each with firearm specifications and aggravating circumstances specifications (capital offense); one count of receiving stolen property; and one count of grand theft. Yarbrough was indicted on the same charges. Herring's case was the first to be tried (*State v. Herring*).

Both Herring and Yarbrough provided audiotaped statements to the police. Though at times contradictory and inconsistent, the tapes clearly indicted both of the defendants.

Guilt/Innocence Phase
Of Trial Testimony

At the trial for Nathan Herring, the jury was presented with the physical evidence and the audiotapes. The victim/psychologist testified that Herring, not Yarbrough, was in possession of a large firearm when they robbed her; Yarbrough had restrained her and told her that they would not hurt her if she cooperated. She also testified that Yarbrough repeatedly stated to Herring, "Don't kill her." She described Herring as "angry" and "jumpy." There was no evidence proving Herring to be the actual shooter. There was also no evidence proving that Herring forced the boys into committing oral sex. Defense attorneys called Yarbrough to testify, but, after being sworn in, he stated, "On advice of my accountant, I invoke the Fifth Commitment Rights [sic]."

The jury found Herring guilty of all charges with the exception of gross sexual imposition. Though both were equally culpable, the jury determined that Herring was not the principal offender in the shooting.

Defense Mitigation Strategy

The defense attorneys' strategy at mitigation was twofold. First, they admitted that Herring was responsible for the aggravated murder, robbery, and kidnappings. Second, they hoped that the jury would find Herring not guilty of the gross sexual imposition charge and find that he was not the principal offender. Having succeeded on these points, the attorneys then focused on other mitigating issues.

The attorneys argued that Nathan had no prior criminal record, which speaks to Ohio's specific mitigating factor: "the offender's lack of a significant history of prior criminal convictions and delinquency adjudications." The attorneys also addressed Nathan's age, 19, which is another statutory factor: "the youth of the offender." Finally, the attorneys focused on Nathan Herring's background and character, the unique circumstances of his life that led him to his current predicament.

Background Information
On Nathan Herring

Nathan "Boo" Herring was the third of three sons born to Monica and Nathan Herring, Sr. His parents separated and divorced when Nathan was very young. Monica had a series of boyfriends and drug abuse problems. Nathan, Sr. has been fairly stable through much of his adult life, though he reported a prior drug problem. He remarried and worked throughout his life. Both parents lived in Steubenville. The oldest son, James, was approximately 23 at the time of the trial. The middle son, Ricky, was deceased. His death had a major impact on the family and on Nathan, Jr.

Nathan "Boo" had a relatively uneventful upbringing until he was approximately 12 years old. According to his family, he did fairly well in school, including making the honor roll several times. He was a gifted athlete and a track and field champion with the Amateur Athletic Union (AAU). According to his coaches and teachers, he had the ability to play professional basketball.

The family's dynamics changed when Nathan was 12. He had qualified to go the National Amateur Athletic Union's Track and Field meet in Baton Rouge, Louisiana. The family worked very hard to raise the money for him to attend the event. On the way down to Louisiana, Monica and her other two sons (Nathan had gone earlier) stopped in Batesville, Mississippi for the night. The boys went for a swim. Ricky, who was the "star" of the family and the most charismatic, drowned. His death devastated the family. As a result, Nathan did not compete in the AAU Nationals. He blamed himself for his brother's death and believed that had he not qualified, Ricky, his closest friend, would not have died.

Following Ricky's death, Monica became quite despondent and unresponsive to Nathan. She began abusing drugs and spent 6 months in prison for a drug offense. Nathan, Sr. had started a second family and as a result Nathan, Jr. felt neglected by both parents. Nathan's schoolwork deteriorated, and he began to hang with a delinquent crowd. By age 13, he was using marijuana. Over the next few years, in part as a result of a serious athletic injury, Nathan stopped participating in any organized activities.

A year before the offense, Nathan met Terrell "Rail" Yarbrough. Rail impressed Boo as a streetwise, "well-draped" (nice clothes), and fun guy to be with. Rail told Boo that he was from New York (a lie) and that he knew many rap stars (another lie). He said that he would introduce Boo to these stars. Boo quickly developed a close relationship with Rail and began selling drugs with him. On the night of the crime, Rail told Boo that he knew of an easy "lick" (burglary). He had met these two college kids before and stated that he had sold marijuana to them and that they owed him money. Boo was only to be the "look-out," but the plan went awry when a third roommate showed up.

Psychological Testing
For Nathan Herring

On the third edition of the Wechsler Adult Intelligence Scale (WAIS-III), Nathan scored a verbal IQ of 83, a performance IQ of 87 resulting in a full scale IQ of 83. This places him in the low average range of intelligence at approximately the 13th percentile.

On the second edition of the Minnesota Multiphasic Personality Inventory, Nathan produced a valid profile. There was no attempt to distort his perception of reality or to overestimate pathology. His profile does indicate a rather uneven to limited level of verbal sophistication. He tests as withdrawn, lacking in self-confidence, and one who tends to avoid close personal involvement. Additionally, his profile is often associated with broken homes and unfavorable family backgrounds that are lacking in normal socializing and maturing experiences. As a result, individuals with this profile are often diagnosed with acute identity disorganization of adolescence. Finally, he is not elevated on scales normally associated with adult criminal behavior (Scale 4).

Mitigation Phase of the Trial

At the mitigation phase of the trial, witnesses included former teachers, coaches, family members, close friends, and a forensic psychologist. Psychological testimony focused on Herring's level of intellectual and emotional functioning, as well as on his particular family dynamics. The psychologist testified about Herring's relationship with both his deceased brother, Ricky, as well as with his friend, "Rail."

Finally, in an unsworn statement not subject to cross-examination (permitted under Ohio law at sentencing), Herring talked about his relationship to his family and to Yarbrough. He accepted full responsibility for the murders of Brian Muha and Aaron Land. He did not blame Yarbrough for the crimes.

The jury returned a verdict of life without the possibility of parole.

The Trial of Terrell Yarbrough

Terrell Yarbrough was tried several months after Herring's trial. The guilt/innocence phase of the trial was very similar to Herring's. The jury returned a guilty verdict on all charges including gross sexual imposition. Mitigation for Yarbrough focused on his neurological impairment and on his family dynamics.

Background Information
On Terrell Yarbrough
(Based on a Neuropsychological Report)

Terrell came from a highly dysfunctional family. His mother admitted at trial that she was a drug user and had been in and out of jail. Terrell's father was an alcoholic and heroin user who had died from AIDS. Terrell's school history is significant for longstanding behavior and conduct problems resulting in significant contact with the juvenile courts. He reported occasional use of alcohol and marijuana.

Neuropsychological testing showed that Terrell had a verbal IQ of 69, a performance IQ of 71 resulting in a full scale IQ of 70 (WAIS-III). His ability to make complex decisions was limited. Although his cognitive skills were not sufficiently impaired to warrant a diagnosis of mental retardation, they did fall far below expectations. Moreover, Mr. Yarbrough demonstrated poor reasoning and planning abilities, as well as a restricted capacity for behavioral inhibition. His history suggested that he probably met the criteria for a diagnosis of attention-deficit/hyperactivity disorder, as well as other psychiatric disorders. Thus, Mr. Yarbrough was likely to behave impulsively, without considering the consequences of his actions. He tended to be concrete in his thinking, and his actions were more likely to be based on his immediate needs rather than on reasoned decisions. He would unlikely be able to function independently, not only because his vocational prospects were very limited but also because he was unable to manage adult responsibilities (selected from court records).

The jury returned a verdict of death. Yarbrough's appeals, at the time of this writing, were based on an *Atkins'* claim of mental retardation. *The New York Times* has taken an interest in his case (see Talbot, 2003).

Chapter 13

ETHICAL ISSUES IN CAPITAL LITIGATION

Clinicians who perform evaluations and assessments in capital cases must be aware of the ethical and legal requirements sanctioned by the states in which they practice and by their own professional organizations. As has been stated previously, capital litigation may last beyond 20 years. Evaluations performed prior to the trial may be reviewed at any of the appellate stages previously discussed. It is, therefore, important that the forensic evaluation be performed in a manner consistent with the standards of the profession. Though these standards may change over time, there is an ethical and legal obligation to obtain informed consent, to maintain records, and to advise the client of the limits of confidentiality. Though state laws may permit the "destruction" of records after a period of time (usually 12 years), records should never be destroyed or altered in capital litigation because these records often form the basis for appellate review. Even after an execution, records should be maintained for any future litigation such as wrongful death.

INFORMED CONSENT AND CONFIDENTIALITY

In many ways, working on capital cases is no different than working on noncapital cases. A psychologist engaged in any type of forensic work is obliged to follow the Specialty Guidelines for Forensic Psychologists (1991) as well as the Ethical Principles of Psychologists and Code of Conduct (American Psychological Association, 2002). But there are other matters that a forensic evaluator must confront in death penalty litigation. The testimony from a psychologist or psychiatrist could convince a jury to recommend the death penalty. Therefore, forensic psychologists have a duty to communicate to the defendant (see *Estelle* *v. Smith*) that he or she is consenting to an evaluation that is not confidential and that the information obtained may be subject to both direct and cross-examination throughout the course of the trial and posttrial period. Such testimony could result in the death penalty even if the evaluator is retained by the defense or appointed to assist the defense. The Specialty Guidelines for Forensic Psychologists* (1991) offers some guidance on this issue:

IV. E.   Forensic psychologists have an obligation to ensure that prospective clients are informed of their legal rights with respect to the anticipated forensic service, of the purposes of any evaluation, of the nature of the procedures to be employed, of the intended uses of any product of their services, and of the party who has employed the forensic psychologist.

IV. E. 1. Unless court ordered, forensic psychologists obtain the informed consent of the client or party, or their legal representative, before proceeding with such evaluations and procedures. If the client appears unwilling to proceed after receiving a thorough notification of the purposes, methods, and intended uses of the forensic evaluation, the evaluation should be postponed and the psychologist should take steps to place the client in contact with his/her attorney for the purpose of legal advice on the issue of participation.

V. A.   Forensic psychologists have an obligation to be aware of the legal standards that may affect or limit the confidentiality or privilege that may attach to their services or their products (see also Guideline IV E), and they conduct their professional activities in a manner that respects those known rights and privileges.

V. B.   Forensic psychologists inform their clients of the limitations to the confidentiality of their services and their products (see also Guideline IV E) by providing them with an understandable statement of their rights, privileges, and the limitations of confidentiality.

The American Psychological Association's Ethical Principles of Conduct and Code of Ethics (2002) outlines the requirements for informed consent and confidentiality:

* From "Specialty Guidelines for Forensic Psychologists," 1991, *Law and Human Behavior*, 15(6), pp. 659-660. Copyright © 1991 by the American Psychology-Law Society/Division 41 of the American Psychological Assoiciation and Kluwer Academic/Plenum Publishers. Reprinted with permission.

3.10 Informed Consent

(a) When psychologists conduct research or provide assessment, therapy, counseling, or consulting services in person or via electronic transmission or other forms of communication, they obtain the informed consent of the individual or individuals using language that is reasonably understandable to that person or persons except when conducting such activities without consent is mandated by law or governmental regulation or as otherwise provided in this Ethics Code.

(b) For persons who are legally incapable of giving informed consent, psychologists nevertheless (1) provide an appropriate explanation, (2) seek the individual's assent, (3) consider such persons' preferences and best interests, and (4) obtain appropriate permission from a legally authorized person, if such substitute consent is permitted or required by law. When consent by a legally authorized person is not permitted or required by law, psychologists take reasonable steps to protect the individual's rights and welfare.

(c) When psychological services are court ordered or otherwise mandated, psychologists inform the individual of the nature of the anticipated services, including whether the services are court ordered or mandated and any limits of confidentiality, before proceeding.

4.01 Maintaining Confidentiality

Psychologists have a primary obligation and take reasonable precautions to protect confidential information obtained through or stored in any medium, recognizing that the extent and limits of confidentiality may be regulated by law or established by institutional rules or professional or scientific relationship.

COMPETENCE

Though it is not necessary for psychologists to be lawyers, Melton et al. (1997) have pointed out that forensic examiners need specialized training in their areas of competency. They also need to be sensitive to a variety of legal principles and procedures as well as to their own code of professional ethics. With regard to forensic activities, the American Psychological Association (2002) Ethical Principles of Conduct and Code of Ethics states

2.01 Boundaries of Competence

(a) Psychologists provide services, teach, and conduct research with populations and in areas only within the boundaries of their competence, based on their education, training, supervised experience, consultation, study, or professional experience. . . .

(f) When assuming forensic roles, psychologists are or become reasonably familiar with the judicial or administrative rules governing their roles.

BIAS AGAINST
THE DEATH PENALTY

Unlike other forensic evaluations, a psychologist's or psychiatrist's attitudes about the death penalty are likely to emerge during the course of testimony. Should such attitudes preclude one from accepting a referral in a capital case? If one has strong feelings against the death penalty, can one still be unbiased, objective, and professional? If one strongly supports the death penalty in a particularly heinous crime, can one be equally unbiased in performing an evaluation or testifying for the state? This issue was raised in the *American Psychology-Law Society Newsletter* (Spring of 2001). Mark Cunningham and Alan Goldstein were invited to respond to this question. Cunningham stated, "Objectivity is enhanced in mitigation evaluations, as in any forensic assessment, by seeking corroborating data from records and third party interviews." He goes on to say, "At capital sentencing . . . the psychologist is not an advocate for the referring party. Rather the forensic psychologist advocates for the clinical and empirical data that are responsive to the referral question" (Goldstein, 2001, pp. 8-9).

On a related ethical matter, anyone who has worked on capital cases has likely encountered the notion of a "defense team" which includes the defense attorneys, mitigation specialists, psychologists, psychiatrists, sociologists, cultural experts, and so on. There is perhaps an expectation that one be a "team" player and only put forward those factors that are helpful to the defendant and ignore those factors that are detrimental. Goldstein stated, "While the good team player may overlook this information, the forensic psychologist must not submit to the pressure or temptation to do so. Our code of ethics as well as the nature of the oath forbids us to do so. In fact, our credibility rests on our objectivity, thoroughness, and fairness. Ultimately it is the attorney's decision to have us submit a report or call us to the stand having weighed the positive and negative information we will convey to the trier-of-fact. . . . To view capital cases as an exception to the rule of providing honest, all-inclusive testimony represents a decision totally unsupported by our profession" (Goldstein, 2001, p. 14).

Therefore, strong feelings about the death penalty (and it is hard not to have strong feelings one way or the other) do not necessarily result in a biased evaluation, though this issue may be the subject of *voir dire* during testimony. One can expect questions like the following:

Prosecutor:	Doctor Smith, isn't it a fact that you are opposed to the death penalty?
Doctor:	Yes.
Prosecutor:	Under any circumstances, correct?
Doctor:	Yes, I suppose.
Prosecutor:	Is there any circumstance in which you believe that a defendant should get the death penalty?
Doctor:	Probably not.
Prosecutor:	Yet you are telling this jury that your strong, unequivocal opposition to the death penalty does not bias you?

Usually, the prosecutor will then follow with a hypothetical example of a heinous murder and force the witness to testify if he or she would or would not support the death penalty. Obviously, the prosecutor has made his or her point. Though defense counsel may object to this line of questioning, most courts are likely to permit this type of cross-examination to let the juries know whether the expert is biased. Jurors have a right to know if a witness has a particular bias that may affect his or her testimony. Expert witnesses must be able to handle this type of cross-examination.

Realistically, psychologists have opinions about all kinds of matters related to litigation. Yet, in this one instance (i.e., capital punishment), it is plausible that the testimony of a psychologist would result in the defendant's being sentenced to death. Or a psychologist could conceivably assist in the restoration of an incompetent defendant in order for him or her to proceed to be executed. Clearly, these issues present moral dilemmas not present in other areas of forensic practice.

RECOMMENDATIONS

Prior to accepting appointment to a capital case, a psychologist should first gain some experience in capital litigation. The psychologist must be familiar with the statutory language describing both aggravating and mitigating factors, the process of death qualification of jurors, and some of the ethical dilemmas. One should have some familiarity with the landmark cases in capital punishment as well as the particular local issues. For example, Texas statute permits testimony about future dangerousness, a question which the jurors must answer (see *Jurek v. Texas*). One should therefore be familiar with the research on the strengths and limitations of risk assessment and be able to critique or perform such an assessment. The psychologist (or any other interested mental health professional) should ask a colleague experienced in the field of capital litigation for permission to "shadow" and observe several cases before accepting an appointment. Any additional training through various workshops in capital litigation is strongly suggested (e.g., American Board of Forensic Psychology's Contemporary Workshop Series). The standards for practicing forensic psychology stress competence. Competence goes beyond "licensure" and is a measurement of both the extent and the boundaries of the psychologist's abilities.

Liebert and Foster (1994) proposed specific standards of practice for mental health evaluations in capital cases. The evaluation should consist of (a) the collection of an accurate medical, developmental, psychological, and social history gathered from multiple sources; (b) a thorough physical and neurological examination; (c) a complete psychiatric and mental status examination; (d) diagnostic studies, including psychometrically based approaches to personality assessment, neuropsychological testing, appropriate brain scans, and blood tests or genetic studies; and (e) the use of other specific specialists and additional appropriate tests as indicated. Though these standards may vary from case to case, at least they provide a basis for the evaluation of a capital defendant as well as an argument to the court for the need for such a thorough evaluation.

Similarly, Cunningham and Reidy (2001) have examined the unique circumstances of evaluating capital defendants and the various dilemmas and perils. They have commented on the errors in violence risk assessment in capital sentencing and in particular the use and misuse of such instruments as the Psychopathy Checklist-Revised (PCL-R; Hare, 2003), the Violence Risk Appraisal Guide (VRAG; Quinsey et al., 1998), and the HCR-20 (Webster et al., 1997). Psychologists who use these instruments in capital cases may be in violation of stated specialty guidelines because elevations on these scales have not been correlated with future dangerousness among American prisoners serving life sentences. One should read the criticisms raised by Cunningham and Reidy (1998b) when considering the utility of these instruments.

Failure to gather all available information and to perform appropriate psychological testing could, therefore, result in an ethical violation and substandard care. Similarly, failure of the lawyer to insist on such a thorough evaluation could result in an allegation of ineffective assistance of counsel under *Strickland* (see *Strickland v. Washington*).

Ethical problems could surface in mental retardation evaluations following *Atkins*. As a result of *Atkins*, many death row defendants are requesting an additional psychological evaluation to determine if they now qualify as a mentally retarded defendant who would no longer be eligible for the death penalty. The difference between mental retardation and borderline intelligence may only be one or two points on the

WAIS-III (Wechsler, 1997; assuming that the defendant also demonstrates impairment in adaptive functioning). Though the evaluation may be "objective," a psychologist with clearly stated concerns or opposition to the death penalty is likely to be viewed as biased by the court. Psychologists should clearly state their views, in such proceedings, to the attorneys (defense attorneys or prosecutors) in order to inform them of any bias — either actual or perceived. A defendant should also be informed of such possible bias that may, in the future, be the subject of court review.

APPENDIX A

KEY AREAS TO EXPLORE IN DEFENDANT'S HISTORY

Complete Educational History of Defendant and Family Members (records, transcripts, awards, sports activities, discipline problems, suspensions, expulsions, etc.)

Complete Family History (grandparents, immigration, migration, etc.)

Defendant's Birth Records and Related Medical Information (birth or delivery complications, illnesses during pregnancy, abuse, etc.)

Defendant's Childhood History, Development, and Family (affection, bonding, neglect, hospitalizations, social service involvement, discipline, etc.)

Defendant's Criminal Record (juvenile and adult, types of offenses, consequences, etc.)

Defendant's Current Charges (details of the crime, relationships with codefendants, drugs or alcohol, etc.)

Defendant's Home Life (pets, environment, entertainment, etc.)

Defendant's Marital History (number of spouses, length of relationships, children, reasons for separation or divorce, etc.)

Defendant's Quality of Life

Description of the Defendant's Neighborhood (all residences, moves, violence, gangs, drugs, etc.)

Employment History (records, promotions, terminations, etc.)

Evidence of Any Severe Mental Illness (hallucinations, delusions, depression, bipolar, suicidal ideation, etc.)

Evidence of Psychological or Sexual Abuse (police reports, names of abusers, etc.)

Evidence of Severe Head Trauma

Evidence of Substance Abuse for Both Defendant and Family

Evidence of Traumatic Experiences (PTSD, violence in the community, etc.)

Family's Criminal History

Family's Financial Situation (assistance, welfare, Aid to Dependant Children, homeless, etc.)

Family's Mental Health History

Military History (records, branch, where served, type of discharge, etc.)

APPENDIX B

FACTS ABOUT THE DEATH PENALTY*

States With the Death Penalty (38)

Alabama	Louisiana	Oregon
Arizona	Maryland	Pennsylvania
Arkansas	Mississippi	South Carolina
California	Missouri	South Dakota
Colorado	Montana	Tennessee
Connecticut	Nebraska	Texas
Delaware	Nevada	Utah
Florida	New Hampshire	Virginia
Georgia	New Jersey	Washington
Idaho	New Mexico	Wyoming
Illinois	New York	*(U.S. Govt.)*
Indiana	North Carolina	*(U.S. Military)*
Kansas	Ohio	
Kentucky	Oklahoma	

---

*Courtesy of the Death Penalty Information Center. Reprinted with permission. This data is frequently updated. For the most current information, go to www.deathpenaltyinfo.org.

States Without the Death Penalty (12)

Alaska	Michigan	West Virginia
Hawaii	Minnesota	Wisconsin
Iowa	North Dakota	(*District of Columbia*)
Maine	Rhode Island	
Massachusetts	Vermont	

Race of Defendants Executed
(Executions Since 1976: Total 905)

White	57%	Hispanic	6%
Black	34%	Other	2%

Race of Death Row Inmates

White	46%	Hispanic	10%
Black	42%	Other	2%

Race of Victims in Death Penalty Cases

White	81%	Hispanic	4%
Black	14%	Other	2%

Death Row Inmates by State*

California	634	South Carolina	76	Washington	11
Texas	458	Mississippi	69	Utah	10
Florida	381	Missouri	60	Illinois	8
Pennsylvania	237	Arkansas	40	Connecticut	7
Ohio	213	Indiana	39	Kansas	7
North Carolina	205	Kentucky	37	(U.S. Military)	7
Alabama	196	Oregon	31	Nebraska	7
Arizona	128	(U.S. Govt.)	28	Montana	5
Georgia	114	Virginia	27	New York	5
Oklahoma	106	Idaho	21	South Dakota	4
Tennessee	104	Delaware	21	Colorado	3
Louisiana	92	New Jersey	15	New Mexico	2
Nevada	89	Maryland	12	Wyoming	1

Total: 3,503

---

*When added, state totals are slightly higher because some inmates are sentenced in more than one state.

Number of Executions by State Since 1976

Texas	322	Arizona	22	Nebraska	3
Virginia	91	Delaware	13	Pennsylvania	3
Oklahoma	73	Illinois	12	Kentucky	2
Missouri	61	Indiana	11	Montana	2
Florida	58	Ohio	11	Oregon	2
Georgia	34	California	10	Colorado	1
North Carolina	31	Nevada	10	Idaho	1
South Carolina	31	Mississippi	6	New Mexico	1
Alabama	28	Utah	6	Tennessee	1
Louisiana	27	Washington	4	Wyoming	1
Arkansas	26	Maryland	3	(*U.S. Govt.*)	3

Total: 910

Executions by Region

South	749	West	60
Midwest	98	Northeast	3

Demographic Characteristics of Prisoners Under Sentence of Death, 2002 (DOJ, November 2003)

Total Number Under Sentence of Death   3,557

Gender

Male	98.6%
Female	1.4%

Education

8th grade or less	14.7%
9th-11th grade	37.1%
High school graduate/GED	38.5%
Any college	9.7%
Median	11th

Marital Status

Married	22.1%
Divorced/Separated	20.8%
Widowed	2.8%
Never Married	54.3%

Age at Time of Arrest for
Capital Offense (from DOJ, 2003)

17 or younger	2.2%
18-19	10.8%
20-24	27.1%
25-29	22.6%
30-34	16.4%
35-39	10.8%
40-44	5.4%
45-49	3.0%
50-54	1.2%
55-59	0.4%
60 and older	0.1%

(40.1 percent% were 24 years old or younger when sentenced)

Average Elapsed Time From Sentence
To Execution (DOJ, 2003)

1977-1983	51 months		1993	113 months
1984	74 months		1994	122 months
1985	71 months		1995	134 months
1986	87 months		1996	125 months
1987	86 months		1997	133 months
1988	80 months		1998	130 months
1989	95 months		1999	143 months
1990	95 months		2000	137 months
1991	116 months		2001	142 months
1992	114 months		2002	127 months

CASES

CASES CITED IN TEXT

Ake v. Oklahoma, 470 U.S. 68 (1985)

Apprendi v. New Jersey, 530 U.S. 466 (2000)

Atkins v. Virginia, 536 U.S. 304 (2002)

Barefoot v. Estelle, 463 U.S. 880 (1983)

Batson v. Kentucky, 476 U.S. 79 (1986)

Betts v. Brady, 316 U.S. 455 (1942)

Booth v. Maryland, 482 U.S. 496 (1987)

Branch v. Texas, No. 69-5031

Bryan v. Moore, 528 U.S. 1133 (2000), No. 99-6723 S.Ct

Burdine v. Johnson, 262 F.3d 336 (2001)

Coker v. Georgia, 433 U.S. 584 (1977)

Douglas v. California, 372 U.S. 353 (1963)

Dusky v. United States, 362 U.S. 402 (1960)

Eddings v. Oklahoma, 455 U.S. 104 (1982)

Enmund v. Florida, 458 U.S. 782 (1982)

Estelle v. Smith, 451 U.S. 454 (1981)

Ford v. Wainwright, 477 U.S. 399 (1986)

Furman v. Georgia, 408 U.S. 238 (1972)

Gideon v. Wainwright, 372 U.S. 335 (1963)

Gilmore v. Utah, 429 U.S. 1012 (1976)

Godinez v. Moran, 509 U.S. 389 (1993)

Gregg v. Georgia, 428 U.S. 155 (1976)

Jackson v. Georgia, No. 69-5030

Johnson v. Zerbst, 304 U.S. 458 (1938)

Jurek v. Texas, 428 U.S. 262 (1976)

Kelly v. S. Carolina, 534 U.S. 246 (2002)

Lockett v. Ohio, 438 U.S. 586 (1978)

Lockhart v. McCree, 476 U.S. 162 (1986)

McCleskey v. Kemp, 481 U.S. 279 (1987)

Miller-El v. Cockrell, 537 U.S. 322 (2003)

Morgan v. Illinois, 504 U.S. 719 (1992)

Murray v. Giarratano, 492 U.S. (1989)

Pate v. Robinson, 383 U.S. 375 (1966)

Payne v. Tennessee, 501 U.S. 808 (1991)

Penry v. Lynaugh, 492 U.S. 302 (1989)

Powell v. Alabama, 287 U.S. 45 (1932)

Proffitt v. Florida, 428 U.S. 242 (1976)

Rees v. Peyton, 384 U.S. 312 (1966)

Riggins v. Nevada, 504 U.S. 127 (1992)

Ring v. Arizona, 536 U.S. 584 (2002)

Roberts v. Louisiana, 428 U.S. 325 (1976)

Sell v. United States, 539 U.S. 166 (2003)

Simmons v. South Carolina, 512 U.S. 154 (1994)

Singleton v. Norris, 124 S.Ct. 74 (2003), 319 F.3d 1018 (2003)

Skipper v. South Carolina, 476 U.S. 1 (1986)

South Carolina v. Gathers, 490 U.S. 805 (1989)

Stanford v. Kentucky, 492 U.S. 361 (1989)

State v. Berry, 1993 Ohio App. LEXIS 5101

State v. Herring, 2002 Ohio 2786

State v. Jones, 2002 Ohio 6914, 2002 Ohio 2074, 2001 Ohio 57

State v. Wilkins, 736 S.W.2d 409 (1987)

Strickland v. Washington, 466 U.S. 668 (1984)

Thompson v. Oklahoma, 487 U.S. 815 (1988)

United States v. Brawner, 471 F.2d 969 (1972)

United States v. McVeigh, 153 F.3d 1166

Wainwright v. Witt, 469 U.S. 412 (1985)

Wiggins v. Smith, 539 U.S. 510 (2003)

Williams v. Taylor, 529 U.S. 362 (2000)

Witherspoon v. Illinois, 391 U.S. 510 (1968)

Woodson v. North Carolina, 428 U.S. 280 (1976)

ADDITIONAL RELEVANT COURT CASES NOT COVERED IN TEXT

Blystone v. Pennsylvania, 494 U.S. 299 (1990)

Brady v. Maryland, 373 U.S. 83 (1963)

Daubert v. Merrell Dow, 113 S.Ct. 2786 (1993)

Emerson v. Gramley, 91 F.3d 898 (7th Cir. 1996)

Harris v. Alabama, 513 U.S. 504 (1995)

Mickens v. Taylor, 535 U.S. 162 (2002)

Tison v. Arizona, 481 U.S. 137, 109 S.Ct. 1676 (1987)

REFERENCES

Allen, M., Mabry, E., & McKelton, D-M. (1998). Impact of juror attitudes about the death penalty on juror evaluation of guilt and punishment: A meta-analysis. *Law and Human Behavior, 22*(6), 715-731.

American Association on Mental Retardation (AAMR). (2002). Definition of Mental Retardation. Retrieved from the AAMR Website: www.aamr.org/Policies/faq_mental_retardation.shtml

American Bar Association. (2003). ABA Guidelines for the Appointment and Performance of Defense Counsel in Death Penalty Cases (rev. ed.). *Hofstra Law Review, 31,* 913-1090.

American Psychiatric Association. (2000). *Diagnostic and Statistical Manual of Mental Disorders* (4th ed. txt. rev.). Washington, DC: Author.

American Psychological Association. (2002, December). Ethical Principles of Psychologists and Code of Conduct. *American Psychologist, 57*(12), 1060-1073.

Banner, S. (2002). *The Death Penalty: An American History.* Cambridge, MA: Harvard University Press.

Bedau, H. A. (1997). *The Death Penalty in America: Current Controversies.* New York: Oxford University Press.

Bennett, C., & Hirschhorn, R. (1993). *Bennett's Guide to Jury Selection and Trial Dynamics in Civil and Criminal Litigation.* St. Paul, MN: West Publishing Co.

Berns, W. (1979). *For Capital Punishment.* New York: Basic Books.

Brown, L., & Leigh, J. E. (2000). *Adaptive Behavior Inventory.* Austin, TX: PRO-ED, Inc.

Bureau of Justice Statistics. (2003). *Homicide Trends in the United States: 2000 Update* (NCJ 197471). Washington, DC: U.S. Department of Justice.

Butler, B. M., & Moran, G. (2002). The role of death qualification in venirepersons' evaluations of aggravating and mitigating circumstances in capital trials. *Law and Human Behavior, 26*(2), 175-184.

Cleckley, H. (1964). *The Mask of Sanity* (4th ed.). St. Louis: Mosby.

Costanzo, M., & White, L. T. (1994). An overview of the death penalty and capital trials: History, current status, legal procedures, and cost. *Journal of Social Issues, 50*(2), 1-18.

Cunningham, M. D. (2003, September). *The Role of the Forensic Psychologist in Death Penalty Litigation.* Cincinnati, OH: American Academy of Forensic Psychology Workshop Series.

Cunningham, M. D. (in press). Special issues in capital sentencing. In M. A. Conroy, P. Lyons, & P. Kwartner (Eds.), *Forensic Evaluations Under Texas Law: Selected Criminal Issues.*

Cunningham, M. D., & Reidy, T. (1998a). Antisocial personality disorder and psychopathy: Diagnostic dilemmas in classifying patterns of antisocial behavior in sentencing evaluations. *Behavioral Sciences and the Law, 16*, 331-351.

Cunningham, M. D., & Reidy, T. (1998b). Integrating base rate data in violence risk assessments at capital sentencing. *Behavioral Sciences and the Law, 16*, 71-95.

Cunningham, M. D., & Reidy, T. (2001). A matter of life and death: Special considerations and heightened practice standards in capital sentencing evaluations. *Behavioral Sciences and the Law, 19*, 473-490.

Cunningham, M. D., & Vigen, M. P. (1999). Without appointed counsel in capital postconviction proceedings: The self-representation competency of Mississippi Death Row inmates. *Criminal Justice and Behavior, 26*, 293-321.

Death Penalty Information Center. www.deathpenaltyinfo.org

Diamond, S. (1993). Instructing on death. *American Psychologist, 48*, 423-434.

Edens, J., Petrila, J., & Buffington, J. (2001, Winter). Psychopathy and the death penalty: Can the Psychopathy Checklist-Revised identify offenders who represent "a continuing threat to soeiety?" *The Journal of Psychiatry and Law, 29*, 433-481.

Elliot, R., & Robinson, R. (1991). Death penalty attitudes and the tendency to convict or acquit: Some data. *Law and Behavior, 15*(4), 389-404

Ellis, J., & Luckasson, R. (1985, March-May). Symposium on the ABA criminal justice mental health standards: Mentally retarded criminal defendants. *George Washington Law Review, 53,* 414.

Ellsworth, P., Bukaty, R., Cown, C., & Thompson, W. (1984). The death-qualified jury and the defense of insanity. *Law and Human Behavior, 8*(1.2), 81-94.

Eysenck, H. J. (1977). *Crime and Personality* (3rd ed.). London: Routledge and Kegan Paul.

Frank, J., & Applegate, B. K. (1998). Assessing juror understanding of capital-sentencing instructions. *Crime and Delinquency, 44*(3), 412-433.

Gacono, C. (2000). *The Clinical and Forensic Assessment of Psychopathy: A Practitioner's Guide.* Mahwah, NJ: Lawrence Erlbaum Associates.

Garvey, S. P. (1998). "Aggravation and mitigation in capital cases: What do jurors think?" *Columbia Law Review, 98,* 1538-1570.

Goldstein, A. (2001, Spring). Objectivity in capital cases. *American Psychology-Law Society Newsletter, 21,* 8-9, 14.

Hare, R. (1965). A conflict and learning theory analysis of psychopathic behavior. *Journal of Research in Crime and Delinquency, 2,* 12-19.

Hare, R. (1970). *Psychopathy: Theory and Research.* New York: John Wiley and Sons.

Hare, R. (2003). Hare Psychopathy Checklist-Revised (PCL-R): 2nd Edition. Toronto, Canada: Multi-Health Systems, Inc.

Hawkins, J. D., Herrenkohl, T. J., Farrington, D. P., Brewer, D., Catalono, R. F., Harachi, T. W., & Cothern, L. (2000, April). Predictors of youth violence. *Juvenile Justice Bulletin.* U.S. Department of Justice, Office of Justice Programs, Office of Juvenile Justice and Delinquency Prevention.

Heilbrun, K. S. (1987). The assessment of competency for execution: An overview. *Behavioral Sciences and the Law, 5,* 383-396.

Heilbrun, K. S., Marczyk, G. R., & DeMatteo, D. (2002). *Forensic Mental Health Assessment: A Casebook.* New York: Oxford University Press.

Johns, J., & Quay, H. (1962). The effect of social reward on verbal conditioning in psychopathic and neurotic military offenders. *Journal of Consulting Psychology, 26*(3), 217-220.

Kanaya, T., Scullin, M. H., & Ceci, S. (2003). The Flynn effect and U.S. policies: The impact of rising IQ scores on American society via mental retardation diagnoses. *American Psychologist, 58*(10), 778-790.

Kovera, M. B., Dickinson, J. J., & Cutler, B. L. (2003). Voir dire and jury selection. In A. Goldstein (Ed.), *Handbook of Psychology – Vol. 11 Forensic Psychology* (pp. 161 - 175). New York: John Wiley and Sons.

Kronenwetter, M. (2001). *Capital Punishment* (2nd ed.). Santa Barbara, CA: ABC-CLOI, Inc.

Latzer, B. (1998). *Death Penalty Cases: Leading U.S. Supreme Court Cases on Capital Punishment*. Boston, MA: Butterworth-Heinemann.

Laurence, J. (1932). *A History of Capital Punishment*. Port Washington, NY: Kennikat Press.

Liebert, D., & Foster, D. (1994). The mental health evaluation in capital cases: Standards of practice. *American Journal of Forensic Psychiatry, 15*(4), 43-64.

Lindner, R. M. (1944). *Rebel Without a Cause*. New York: Grove Press.

Loftus, E. F. (1996). *Eyewitness Testimony* (2nd ed). Cambridge, MA: Harvard University Press.

Loftus, E. F., & Ketcham, K. (1994). *The Myth of Repressed Memory*. New York: St. Martin's Press.

Luginbuhl, J., & Middenhorf, K. (1988). Death penalty beliefs and jurors' responses to aggravating and mitigating circumstances in capital trials. *Law and Human Behavior, 12*(3,) 263-280.

Lynch, M., & Haney, C. (2000). Discrimination and instructional comprehension: Guided discretion, racial bias, and the death penalty. *Law and Human Behavior, 24*(3), 337-358.

Mailer, N. (1959). *Advertisements for Myself*. New York: Putnam.

Maughs, S. (1941). A conception of the psychopathic personality. *Journal of Criminal Psychopathology, 2*, 329-356.

Mednick, S. (1977). A bio-social theory of the learning of law-abiding behavior. In S. A. Medick & K. O. Christiansen (Eds.), *Biosocial Bases of Criminal Behavior* (pp. 1-8). New York: Gardner Press.

Meloy, J. R. (1988). *The Psychopathic Mind: Origins, Dynamics, and Treatment*. Northvale, NJ: Jason Aronson.

Meloy, J. R. (1992). *Violent Attachments*. Northvale, NJ: Jason Aronson.

Meloy, J. R. (1995). Antisocial personality disorder. In G. Gabbard (Ed.), *Treatments of Psychiatric Disorders* (2nd ed.) (Vol. II, pp. 2273-2290). Washington, DC: American Psychiatric Press.

Melton, G. B., Petrila, J., Poythress, N. G., & Slobogin, C. (1997). *Psychological Evaluations for the Courts: A Handbook for Mental Health Professionals and Lawyers* (2nd ed.). New York: Guilford Press.

Nihira, K., Leland, H., & Lambert, N. (1993). *The Adaptive Behavior Scale-Residential and Community (ABS-RC:2)*. Austin, TX: PRO-ED (published by the American Association on Mental Retardation).

Norton, L. (1992). Capital cases: Mitigation investigations. *The Champion, 4*, 35-43.

Pfefferman, N. (2003, March 10). Jews and the death penalty. *The Jewish Journal*, on-line at www.jewishjournal.com/old/deathpenalty 2.3.10.0.htm

Pinel, P. (1962). *A Treatise on Insanity* (D. P. David, Trans.). New York: Hafner Publishing Co. (Original work published 1806)

Protess, D., & Warden, R. (1998). *A Promise of Justice*. New York: Hyperion.

Quay, H. C. (1965). Psychopathic personality as pathological stimulation seeking. *American Journal of Psychiatry, 122*, 180-183.

Quinsey, V., Harris, G., Rice, M., & Cormier, C. (1998). *Violent Offenders: Appraising and Managing Risk*. Washington, DC: American Psychological Association.

Raine, A. (1993). *The Psychopathology of Crime*. New York: Academic Press.

Randa, L. (1997). *Society's Final Solution: A History and Discussion of the Death Penalty*. Lanham, MD: University Press of America.

Reggio, M. (1997). History of the death penalty. In L. Randa (Ed.), *Society's Final Solution: A History and Discussion of the Death Penalty* (pp. 1-11). Lanham, MD: University Press of America.

Rogers, R., Duncan, J. C., Lynett, E., & Sewell, K. W. (1994). Prototypical analysis of antisocial personality disorder. *Law and Human Behavior, 19*, 474-484.

Schroeder, J. (2003, July-September). Forging a new practice: Social work's role in death penalty litigation investigations. *Families in Society, 84*(3), 423-432.

Silver, R. J., Cirincione, C., & Steadman, H. J. (1994). Demythologizing inaccurate perceptions of the insanity defense. *Law and Human Behavior, 18*, 632-670.

Smalldon, J. (1993). *Antisocial Personality Disorder (APD): A Primer*. Unpublished manuscript.

Sorensen, J., & Pilgrim, R. (2000). An actuarial risk assessment of violence posed by capital murder defendants. *Criminology, 90*(4), 1251-1270.

Sparrow, S. S., Balla, D. A., & Cicchetti, D. V. (1984). *Vineland Adaptive Behavior Scales*. Circle Pines, MN: American Guidance Service.

Specialty Guidelines for Forensic Psychologists. (1991). *Law and Human Behavior, 15*(6), 655-665.

Steinberg, L., & Scott, E. (2003). Less guilty by reason of adolescence: Developmental immaturity, diminished responsibility, and the juvenile death penalty. *American Psychologist, 58*(12), 1009-1018.

Stetler, R. (1999). Why capital cases require mitigation specialists. *The Champion, 1*, 35-40.

Stetler, R., Burt, M., & Johnson, J. (1998). *Mitigation Introduction: Mitigation Evidence Twenty Years After* Lockett. Paper presented at the 26th Annual Public Defender Conference, Lexington, KY.

Talbot, M. (2003, June 29). The executioner's IQ test. *New York Times Magazine*, pp. 30-35, 52, 58-60.

U.S. Department of Justice. (1995, June). Guide for implementing the comprehensive strategy for serious, violent, and chronic juvenile offenders. *Juvenile Justice Bulletin: OJJDP Update on Programs* (NCJ 153571). Washington, DC: Office of Justice Programs, Office of Juvenile Justice and Delinquency Prevention.

U.S. Department of Justice. (2003, November). *Capital Punishment, 2002* (NCJ 201848). Washington, DC: Bureau of Justice Statistics.

Wallace, J., Schmitt, W., Vitale, J., & Newman, J. (2000). Experimental investigation of information-processing deficiencies in psychopaths: Implications for diagnosis and treatment. In C. Gacono (Ed.), *The Clinical and Forensic Assessment of Psychopathy: A Practitioner's Guide* (pp. 87-109). Mahwah, NJ: Lawrence Erlbaum Associates.

Webster, C. D., Douglas, K. S., Eaves, D., & Hart, S. D. (1997). *HCR-20: Assessing Risk for Violence (Version 2)*. Burnaby, Canada: Mental Health, Law, and Policy Institute, Simon Fraser University.

Wechsler, D. (1955). *Manual for the Wechsler Adult Intelligence Scale*. New York: Psychological Corporation.

Wechsler, D. (1958). *The Measurement and Appraisal of Adult Intelligence* (4th ed.). Baltimore: Williams and Wilkins.

Wechsler, D. (1981). *Manual for the Wechsler Adult Intelligence Scale-Revised*. New York: Psychological Corporation.

Wechsler, D. (1974). *Manual for the Wechsler Intelligence Scale for Children-Revised*. San Antonio, TX: Psychological Corporation.

Wechsler, D. (1991). *Wechsler Intelligence Scale for Children-Third Edition*. San Antonio, TX: Psychological Corporation.

Wechsler, D. (1997). *Manual for the Wechsler Adult Intelligence Scale* (3rd ed.). New York: Psychological Corporation.

Wells, G. L. (1995). Scientific study of witness memory: Implications for public and legal policy. *Psychology, Public Policy, and the Law,* 1(4), 726-731.

Wheelan, D. (1996). Investigating the capital case. *The Champion,* 7, 34-39 (on-line). Available at http://www.nacdl.org/CHAMPION/ARTICLES/96jul01.htm

Wrightsman, L. S., Nietzel, M. T., & Fortune, W. H. (1998). *Psychology and the Legal System* (4th ed.). Pacific Grove, CA: Brooks/Cole.

Young, M., Justice, J., Erdberg, P., & Gacono, C. (2000). The incarcerated psychopath in psychiatric treatment. In C. Gacono (Ed.), *The Clinical and Forensic Assessment of Psychopathy: A Practitioner's Guide* (pp. 313-350). Mahwah, NJ: Lawrence Erlbaum Associates.

Zapf, P., Boccaccini, M., & Brodsky, S. (2003). Assessment of competency for execution: Professional guidelines and an evaluation checklist. *Behavioral Sciences and the Law,* 21, 103-120.

INDEX